FIREFLY • POCKET • GUIDES

ANIMALS OF THE WORLD

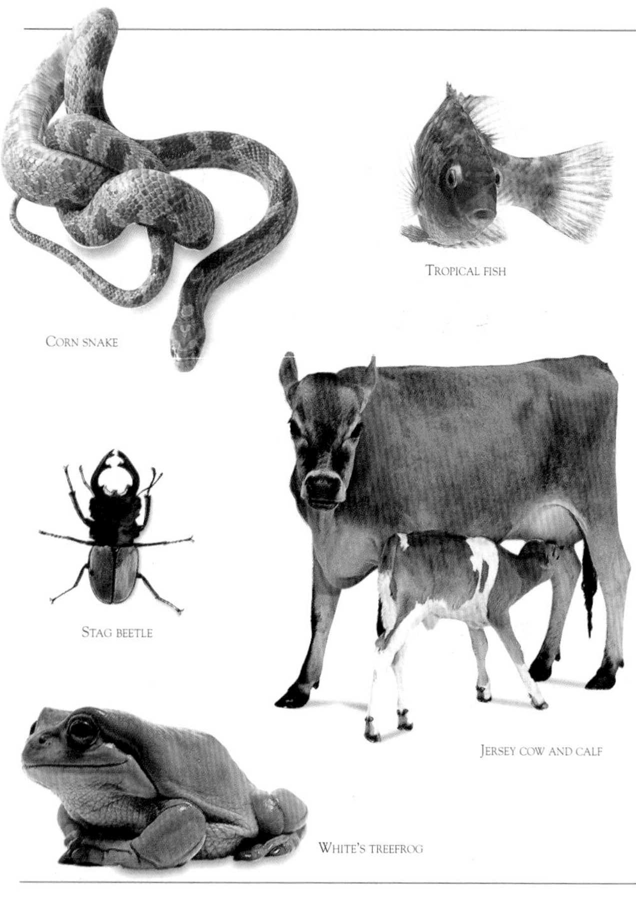
Corn snake

Tropical fish

Stag beetle

Jersey cow and calf

White's treefrog

FIREFLY • POCKET • GUIDES

ANIMALS OF THE WORLD

AMMONITE

CRESTED WATER DRAGON

LESSER FLAMINGO

FIREFLY BOOKS

A DORLING KINDERSLEY BOOK

Published by Firefly Books Ltd. 1999

Writers and consultants:
David Alderton,
Steve Brooks, Dr. Barry Clarke,
John Farndon, Mark Lambert,
Laurence Mound, Scarlett O'Hara,
Barbara Taylor, Steve Parker,
Joyce Pope, David Taylor

Produced for Dorling Kindersley by
PAGE*One*, Cairn House, Elgiva Lane, Chesham,
Buckinghamshire, HP5 2JD

First published in Canada in 1999 by Firefly Books Ltd.
3680 Victoria Park Avenue, Willowdale,
Ontario, Canada M2H 3K1

The material in this book originally appeared in the following
DK Pocket titles: *Birds, Cats, Dogs, Encyclopedia, Horses, Insects, Mammals, Nature Facts, Reptiles, Sharks.*

Canadian Cataloguing in Publication Data

Animals of the world
(Firefly pocket guides)
Includes index.
ISBN 1-55209-412-X

1. Animals – Encyclopedias, Juvenile. I. Series
QL49.A547 1999 j590'.3 C99-930091-1

Color reproduction by Colourscan, Singapore
Printed and bound in Italy by L.E.G.O.

Contents

BIRDWING BUTTERFLY

GREEN MANTELLA

Tawny owl

Armadillo

GREAT DANE

HOW TO USE THIS BOOK

These pages show you how to use the *Firefly Pocket Guides Animals of the World.* The book is divided into seven sections about the animal kingdom. There is also an introductory section about the origins of animal life, and how animals are classified. At the back of the book, there is a comprehensive index.

HEADING AND INTRODUCTION

Every spread has a subject heading. This is followed by the introduction, which outlines the subject and gives a clear idea of what these pages are about.

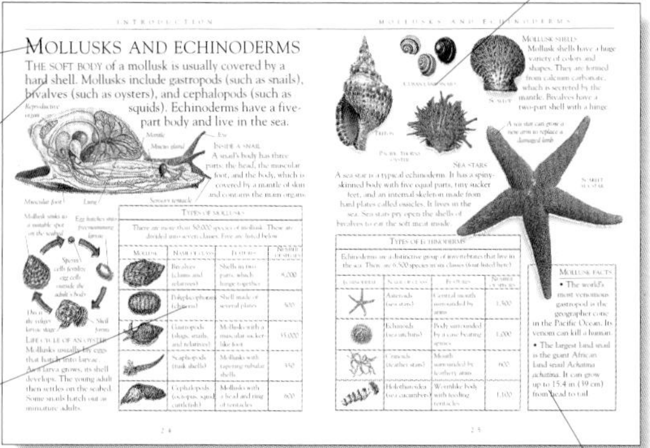

Label

Heading

Introduction

MOLLUSKS AND ECHINODERMS

THE SOFT BODY of a mollusk is usually covered by a hard shell. Mollusks include gastropods (such as snails), bivalves (such as oysters), and cephalopods (such as squids). Echinoderms have a five-part body and live in the sea.

Data box

Fact box

DATA BOX

Some pages have data boxes, which contain detailed numerical information. This box gives data about types of mollusk.

FACT BOXES

Many pages have fact boxes. The information in these is related to the main topic on the page.

LABELS

For clarity, some pictures have labels. These give extra information about the picture, or provide clearer identification.

RUNNING HEADS

Across the top of the pages there are running heads. The lefthand page gives the section, the righthand the subject.

SIZE INDICATORS

In some sections of this book, you will find clear symbols next to photography. These indicate the average size of an animal.

Running head
Size indicator
REAR-FANGED SNAKES
SNAKES WITH FANGS in the back of their mouth are found in both the Old and New Worlds, and, as with other groups of snakes, they vary greatly in color, size, and habitat. They are not as efficient as front-fanged snakes at injecting venom, and so most species are harmless to humans. Large rear-fanged snakes, however, can be dangerous.
IN THE TREETOPS
HIGH UP IN THE RAINFOREST CANOPY it is light and warm and there is plenty of food, especially fruits, seeds, and insect life. Bird life includes large bird predators such as eagles which patrol the treetops looking for prey. Canopy birds, such as parrots and toucans, climb well and have strong feet for grasping branches.
Annotation
Caption

ANNOTATION

Pictures often have extra information around them, which picks out features. This text appears in *italics*, and uses leader lines to point to details.

CAPTIONS

Each illustration in the book is accompanied by a detailed, explanatory caption.

INDEX

There is an index at the back of the book that alphabetically lists every subject. By referring to the index, information on particular topics can be found quickly.

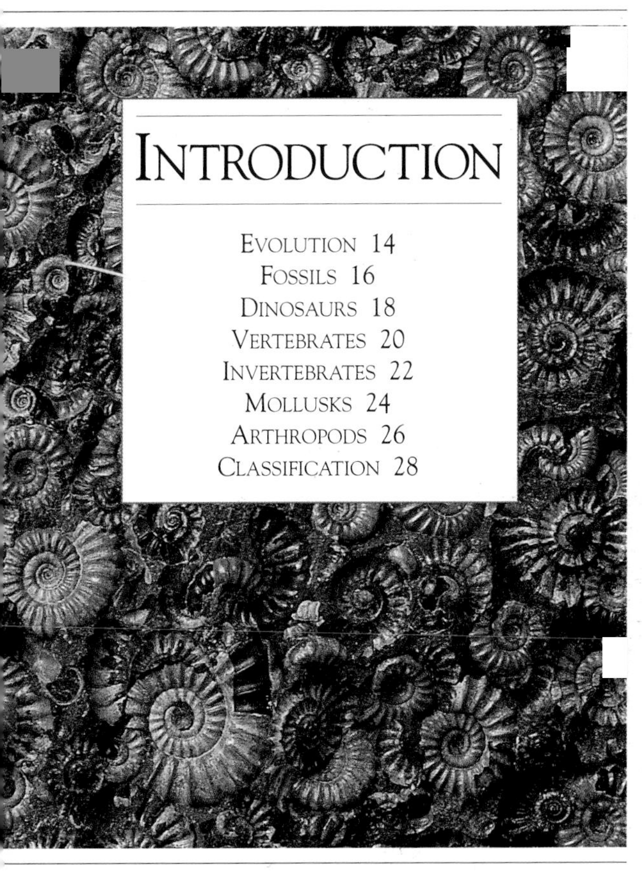

INTRODUCTION

EVOLUTION

SINCE LIFE appeared 3.8 billion years ago, millions of different creatures have come and gone. As habitats changed, some species survived by adapting, while others died out quickly. This gradual turnover of species is called evolution.

PORPOISE'S FRONT FLIPPER

"Finger" bones form a powerful flipper for swimming

Two sets of short "arm" bones

Two sets of long bones make up the arm

Five sets of finger bones make up hand

HUMAN ARM

ADAPTATION

Evolution works by slowly adapting existing features to suit different purposes. Although they look very different, humans and porpoises both have two "arm" bones and five "finger" bones.

LIFE-FORMS THROUGH THE AGES

By working out when certain rocks formed, and then studying the fossils found in them, paleontologists – who study the life-forms of the past – have built up a remarkable picture of the way species have changed since the dawn of the Cambrian period 590 million years ago. Little is known of Precambrian life forms because very few fossils remain.

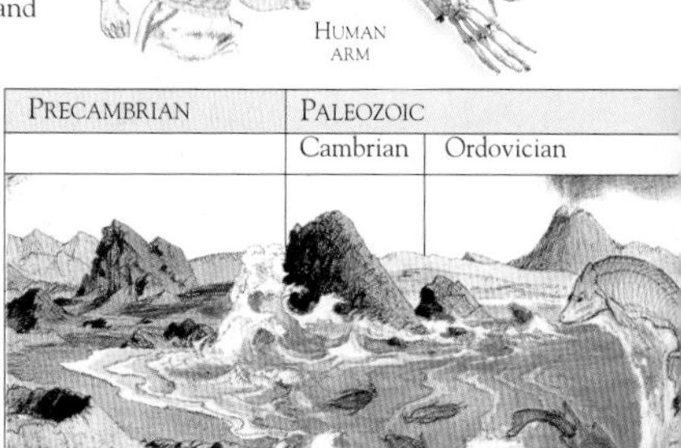

PRECAMBRIAN	PALEOZOIC	
	Cambrian	Ordovician
4600–590 mya Single-celled life-forms such as bacteria and algae appear, then soft multi-celled life-forms, like worms and jellyfish.	*590–505 mya No life on land. Inverterbrates flourish in the seas. First mollusks and trilobites.*	*505–438 mya First crustaceans and early jawless fish appear. Coral reefs form. Sahara glaciated.*

How evolution works

According to Darwin's theory of evolution, animals and plants developed over millions of years, surviving according to their ability to adapt to a changing environment. Until the mid-19th-century, people believed that life-forms did not change since their creation by an omnipotent deity.

Charles Darwin (1809–1882)

The theory of evolution was developed by English naturalist Charles Darwin after studying the animals of the Galápagos Islands. He published his findings in 1859 in his book *On the Origin of Species*.

Evolution of the horse

Eohippus
This hare-sized creature browsed in woodlands.

Mesohippus
Over millions of years, Eohippus evolved into a larger grazing animal.

Merychippus
As early horses adapted to the grasslands, they developed longer limbs to escape from predators.

Modern horse
The horses of today are highly developed grazers; they have long legs for running and sharp senses.

Silurian	Devonian	Carboniferous	Permian
438–408 mya *First jawed fish. Huge sea scorpions hunt in the sea. Small land plants colonize the shore.*	408–355 mya *Age of sharks and fish. Insects and amphibians appear on land. Giant ferns form forests.*	355–290 mya *Warm swampy forests leave remains that will turn to coal. First reptiles.*	290–250 mya *Reptiles diversify, conifers replace tree ferns. Mass extinction as Earth turns cold.*

FOSSILS

THE REMAINS of living things preserved naturally, often for many millions of years, are called fossils. Most fossils are formed in rocks; however, remains can also be preserved in ice, tar, peat, and amber. Fossils tell us nearly all we know about the history of life on Earth.

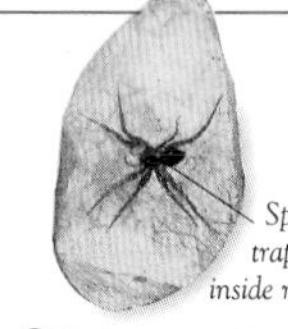

Spider trapped inside resin

SPIDER IN AMBER
Amber is fossilized tree resin that may also preserve trapped insects.

AMMONITES BECAME EXTINCT 65 MYA

Fossilized shell

KINDS OF FOSSILS
Most fossils form on the seabed, so shells and sea creatures are the most common. Fossils of land animals and plants are rarer. Footprints, burrows, or droppings may also be preserved.

MESOZOIC			CENOZOIC	
Triassic	Jurassic	Cretaceous	Tertiary	
			Palaeocene	Eocene
250–205 mya *Mammals and dinosaurs appear. The climate warms and seed-bearing plants dominate.*	*205–135 mya* *The age of the dinosaurs. The first known bird, Archaeopteryx, appears.*	*135–66 mya* *First flowering plants. Period ends with a mass extinction that wipes out dinosaurs.*	*66–53 mya* *Warm, humid climate. Mammals, insects, and flowering plants flourish.*	*53–36 mya* *Mammals grow larger and diversify. Primates evolve.*

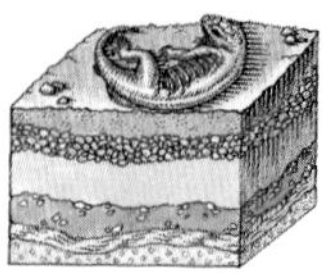

1 ANIMAL DIES
The body of a dead animal lies decaying on the surface of the land.

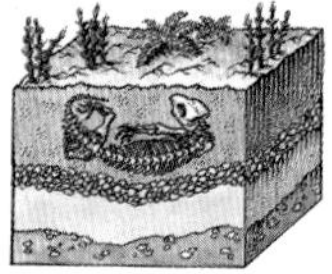

2 REMAINS SINK
Gradually, the body becomes covered with sand or mud.

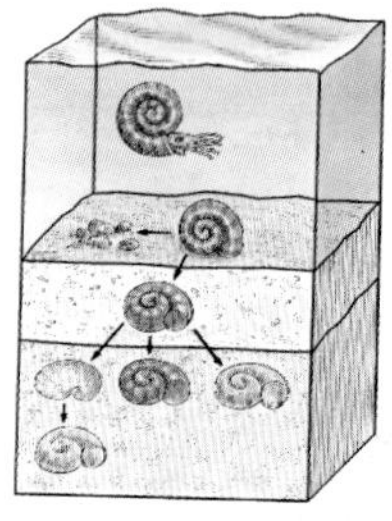

FOSSILIZATION AT SEA
Dead organisms sink to the seabed and are buried. As the sediment turns to rock, their remains are either chemically altered or dissolve to leave a cavity, which may fill with minerals to form a cast.

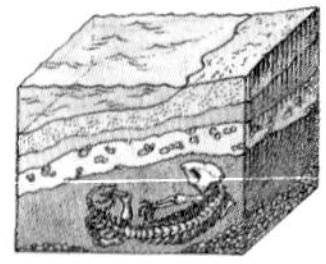

3 BONES ALTER
Over time, the bones are altered, and the sand and mud turn to rock.

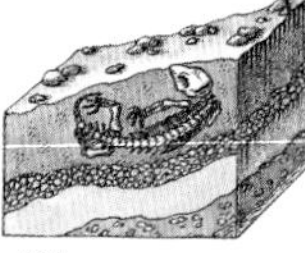

4 FOSSIL IS EXPOSED
Eventually, weather and erosion expose the fossil at the surface.

			Quaternary	
Oligocene	Miocene	Pliocene	Pleistocene	Holocene
36–23 mya First humanlike creatures appear. Hunting birds thrive. Some mammals die out.	*23–6.3 mya Climate cools, and forests shrink. Deerlike hoofed mammals flourish. First hominids.*	*6.3–1.6 mya Cold and dry. Mammals reach maximum diversity. Many modern mammals appear.*	*1.6m–10,000 ya Ice Ages. Homo sapiens evolves. Mammoths and saber-toothed tigers die out.*	*10,000 ya to present Humans develop agriculture and technology. Human activity threatens many species.*

DINOSAURS

FOR 150 MILLION YEARS, Earth was dominated by giant reptiles called dinosaurs, including *Seismosaurus*, the largest creature ever to walk on land. Then, 65 million years ago, all the dinosaurs mysteriously died out.

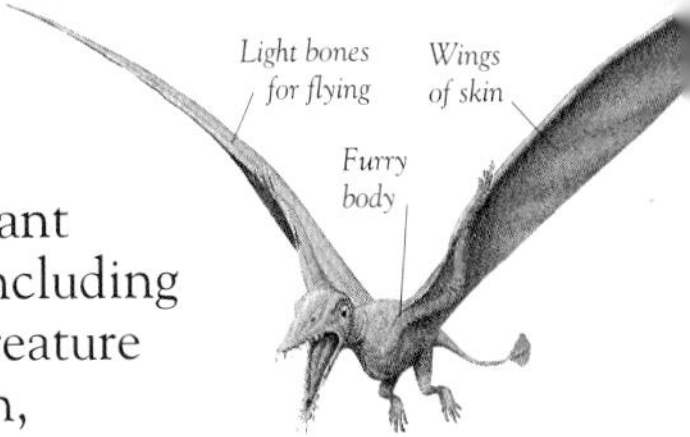

Light bones for flying

Wings of skin

Furry body

PTEROSAUR
While dinosaurs ruled the land, giant reptiles, like Pterosaur, flew in the air.

DINOSAUR GROUPS
Scientists divide dinosaurs into two orders according to the arrangement of their hipbones. Saurischians have lizardlike hips and include both plant and meateaters. Ornithischians have bird-like hips and are all plant eaters. The two orders are divided into five subgroups.

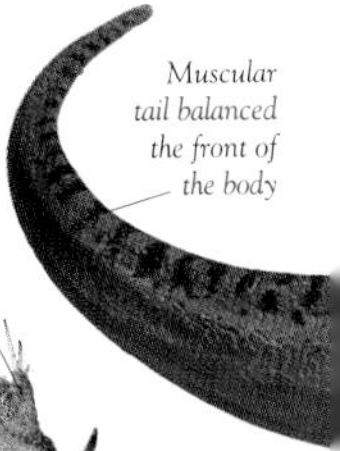

Muscular tail balanced the front of the body

Long neck for browsing in treetops

Ruff

Horn

SALTASAURUS

STYRACOSAURUS

Sauropods (Saurischians) *were huge, long-necked four-legged planteaters.*

Marginocephalians (Saurischians) *had a bony ruff and horns for self-defense.*

TYRANNOSAURUS

STEGOSAURUS

CORYTHOSAURUS

Thyreophorans (Ornithischians) *were spiny-backed planteaters.*

Theropods (Saurischians) *were two-legged meateaters.*

Ornithopods (Ornithischians) *had a horny beak and birdlike feet.*

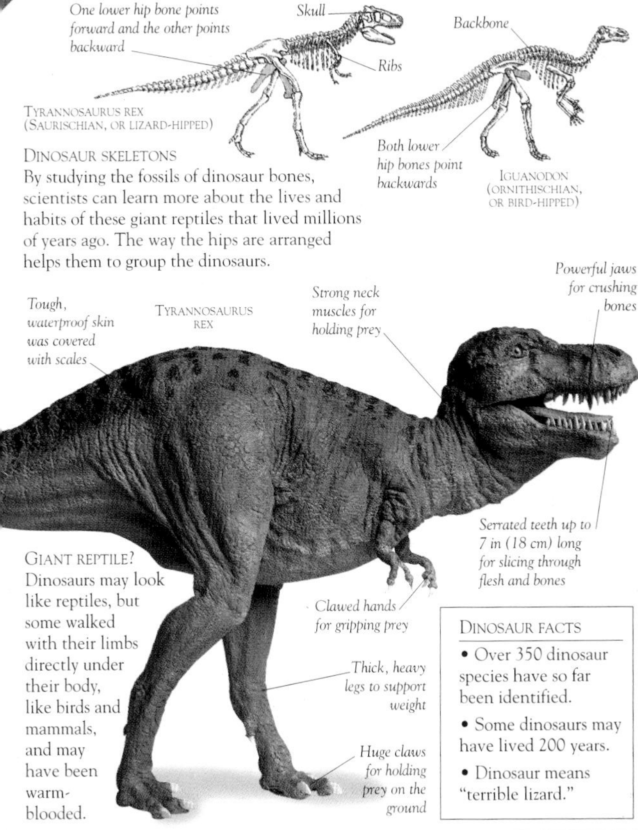

DINOSAUR SKELETONS

By studying the fossils of dinosaur bones, scientists can learn more about the lives and habits of these giant reptiles that lived millions of years ago. The way the hips are arranged helps them to group the dinosaurs.

GIANT REPTILE?

Dinosaurs may look like reptiles, but some walked with their limbs directly under their body, like birds and mammals, and may have been warm-blooded.

DINOSAUR FACTS

- Over 350 dinosaur species have so far been identified.
- Some dinosaurs may have lived 200 years.
- Dinosaur means "terrible lizard."

Vertebrates

GORILLA SKELETON

ONLY ABOUT three percent of all animals have backbones, and these are called vertebrates. There are more than 40,000 different species of vertebrates, divided into classes of mammals, birds, fish, reptiles, and amphibians. Their sense organs and nervous systems are well developed, and they have adapted to almost every habitat.

BACKBONE
Vertebrates have a skeleton of bone, with a backbone, two pairs of limbs, and a skull that protects the brain. Inside are the heart, lungs, and other organs.

REPTILES
Lizards, snakes, crocodiles, and geckos are reptiles. They all have a tough, scaly skin. Young reptiles hatch from eggs, and look like tiny versions of their parents. This chameleon is a type of lizard.

Spines along backbone give protection from attack

Scaly skin

MADAGASCAN CHAMELEON

Female frog lays eggs, called frogspawn

Male fertilizes spawn

ANIMAL REPRODUCTION
In vertebrates, offspring are created when males and females come together and the male's sperm join the female's eggs. This is called sexual reproduction, and usually involves mating. A few animals are neither male nor female, and they reproduce asexually.

Prehensile tail for holding onto branches

SENSES

Mammals and other vertebrate animals have senses to help them find their way, locate food, and avoid enemies. For land animals, such as this caracal, sight, hearing, and smell are the most important senses. Sea creatures rely more on smell and taste to escape danger and find food.

CARACAL

TWINSPOT WRASSE

FISH

With streamlined bodies covered in slippery scales, these vertebrates are perfectly suited to life in the water.

Scales covered in slimy mucus

BIRDS

The only animals that have feathers are birds, and most of them are powerful fliers. Birds have a beak, or bill, instead of teeth, and all reproduce by laying eggs.

COUNT RAGGI'S BIRD OF PARADISE

RED-EYED TREE FROG

Large eyes spot prey

AMPHIBIANS

Frogs, toads, newts, and salamanders are amphibians. These vertebrates spend part of their lives in water and part on land. They all reproduce by laying eggs.

Long legs for jumping

PORCUPINE

Spiny quills protect body

Fur helps keep body warm

MAMMAL

A mammal is usually covered by fur or hair. It gives birth to live young, which it feeds with milk.

INVERTEBRATES

NINE-TENTHS of all animals are invertebrates, which means they have no backbone. They include jellyfish, sponges, starfish, coral, worms, crabs, spiders, and insects.

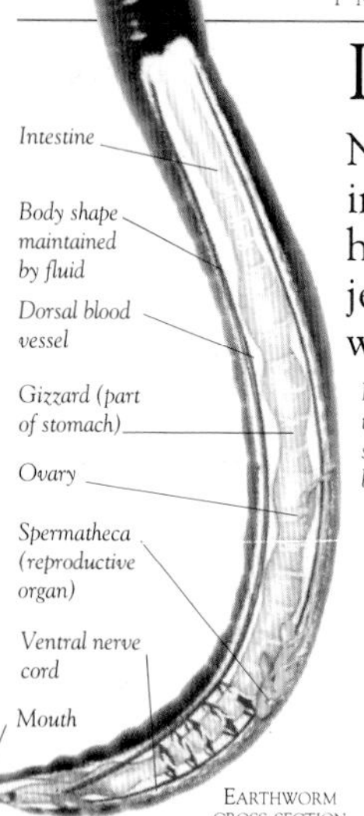

EARTHWORM CROSS-SECTION

MOLLUSKS
These soft-bodied invertebrates are often protected by a hard shell. Most mollusks, such as squid and octopuses, clams, mussels, and scallops, live in water, but some, like snails and slugs, live on land.

WORMS
A worm is an animal with a long soft body and no legs. There are many different kinds, including flatworms, tapeworms, earthworms, roundworms, and leeches.

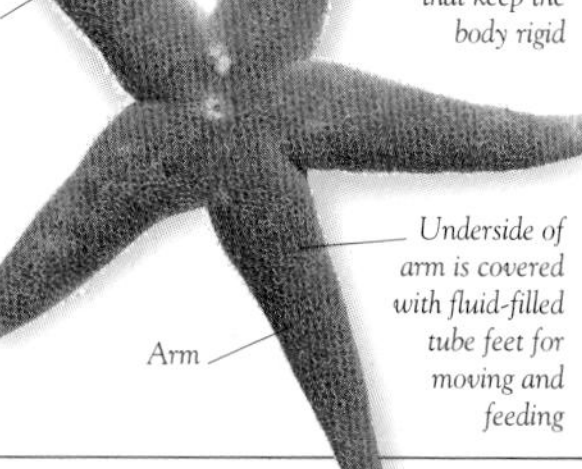

STARFISH AND URCHINS
Starfish, sea urchins, and sea cucumbers are all of echinoderms. All are predators, and most have sucker-tipped "tube feet" through which they pump water to move along and feed. The five broad arms of a starfish can wrench open a shellfish to suck out the contents.

LIFE CYCLE
Each invertebrate has its own life cycle, but most species lay eggs. Some go through several larval stages; others hatch as miniature adults.

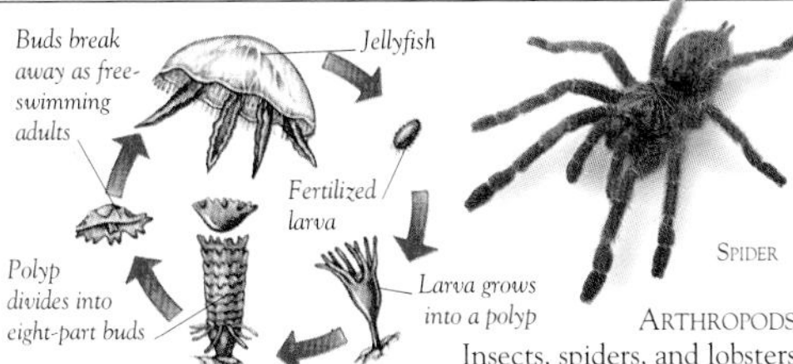

ARTHROPODS
Insects, spiders, and lobsters are all arthropods. They have jointed limbs and a tough external skeleton.

CROSS SECTION OF A JELLYFISH

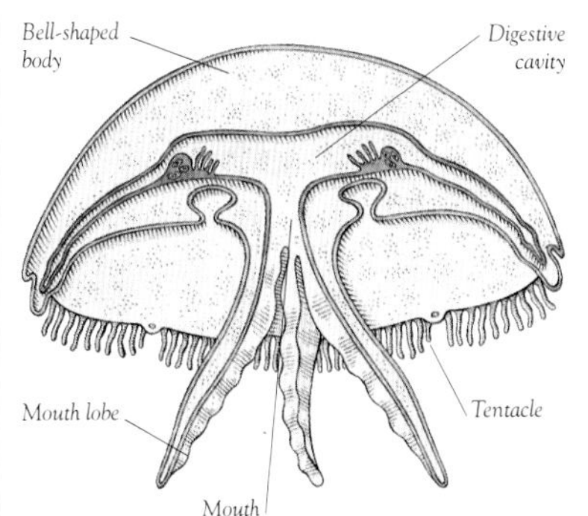

Jellyfish, anemones, and coral are all kinds of coelenterates – sea creatures with a mouth surrounded by tentacles. These tentacles usually carry a stinger to stun or kill prey. Some coelenterates, called polyps, always attach to a solid object, such as a rock; others, called medusas, move by contracting their bell-shaped bodies.

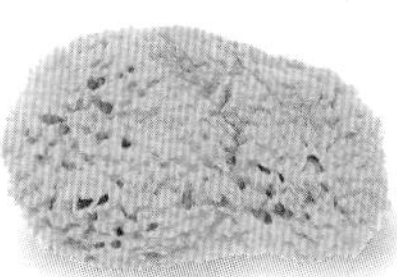

SPONGES
These primitive sea creatures feed by drawing water into the holes in their soft bodies and filtering out any food.

INVERTEBRATE FACTS

- Up to 500 million hookworms may be found in a single human.
- Roundworms are probably the most numerous animals on Earth.

MOLLUSKS AND ECHINODERMS

THE SOFT BODY of a mollusk is usually covered by a hard shell. Mollusks include gastropods (such as snails), bivalves (such as oysters), and cephalopods (such as squids). Echinoderms have a five-part body and live in the sea.

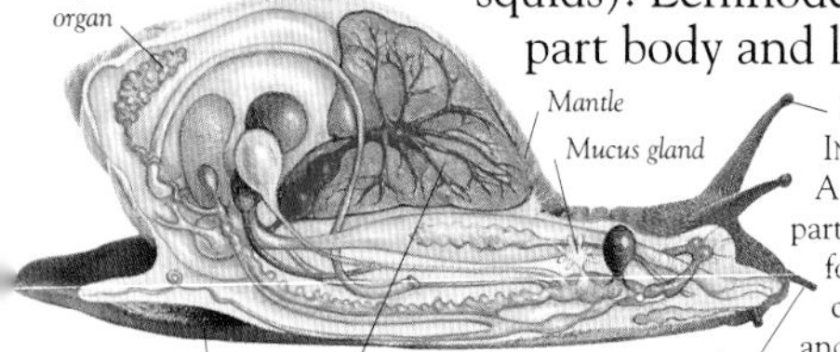

Reproductive organ

Mantle

Eye

Mucus gland

Muscular foot

Lung

Sensory tentacle

INSIDE A SNAIL
A snail's body has three parts: the head, the muscular foot, and the body, which is covered by a mantle of skin and contains the main organs.

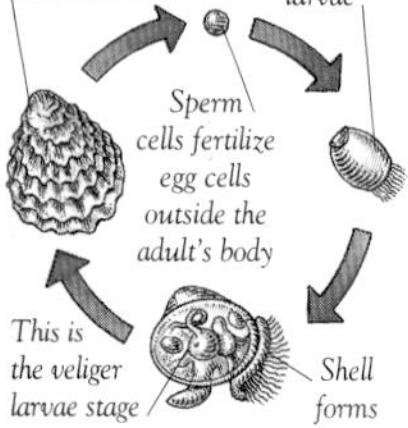

Mollusk sinks to a suitable spot on the seabed

Egg hatches into freeswimming larvae

Sperm cells fertilize egg cells outside the adult's body

This is the veliger larvae stage

Shell forms

LIFE CYCLE OF AN OYSTER
Mollusks usually lay eggs that hatch into larvae. As a larva grows, its shell develops. The young adult then settles on the seabed. Some snails hatch out as miniature adults.

TYPES OF MOLLUSKS

There are more than 50,000 species of mollusk. These are divided into seven classes. Five are listed below.

MOLLUSK	NAME OF CLASS	FEATURES	NUMBER OF SPECIES
	Bivalves (clams and relatives)	Shells in two parts, which hinge together	8,000
	Polyplacophorans (chitons)	Shell made of several plates	500
	Gastropods (slugs, snails, and relatives)	Mollusks with a muscular sucker-like foot	35,000
	Scaphopods (tusk shells)	Mollusks with tapering tubular shells	350
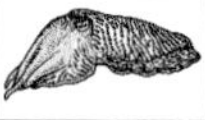	Cephalopods (octopus, squid, cuttlefish)	Mollusks with a head and ring of tentacles	600

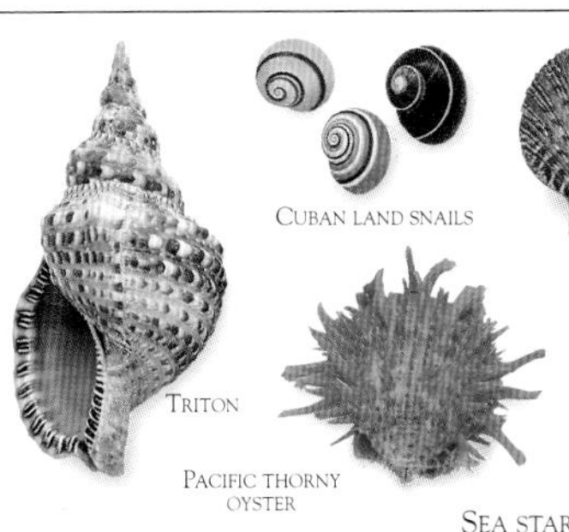

CUBAN LAND SNAILS

TRITON

PACIFIC THORNY OYSTER

SCALLOP

MOLLUSK SHELLS

Mollusk shells have a huge variety of colors and shapes. They are formed from calcium carbonate, which is secreted by the mantle. Bivalves have a two-part shell with a hinge.

A sea star can grow a new arm to replace a damaged limb

SCARLET SEA STAR

SEA STARS

A sea star is a typical echinoderm. It has a spiny-skinned body with five equal parts, tiny sucker feet, and an internal skeleton made from hard plates called ossicles. It lives in the sea. Sea stars pry open the shells of bivalves to eat the soft meat inside.

TYPES OF ECHINODERMS

Echinoderms are a distinctive group of invertebrates that live in the sea. There are 6,500 species in six classes (four listed here).

ECHINODERM	NAME OF CLASS	FEATURES	NUMBER OF SPECIES
	Asteroids (sea stars)	Central mouth surrounded by arms	1,500
	Echinoids (sea urchins)	Body surrounded by a case bearing spines	1,000
	Crinoids (feather stars)	Mouth surrounded by feathery arms	600
	Holothuroidea (sea cucumbers)	Wormlike body with feeding tentacles	1,100

MOLLUSK FACTS

- The world's most venomous gastropod is the geographer cone in the Pacific Ocean. Its venom can kill a human.
- The largest land snail is the giant African land snail *Achatina achatina*. It can grow up to 15.4 in (39 cm) from head to tail.

ARTHROPODS

ARACHNIDS, CRUSTACEANS, and insects are part of the arthropod group of invertebrates. Insects are by far the largest of these three groups. All arthropods have a jointed body with a tough body case. The case is shed as the animal grows.

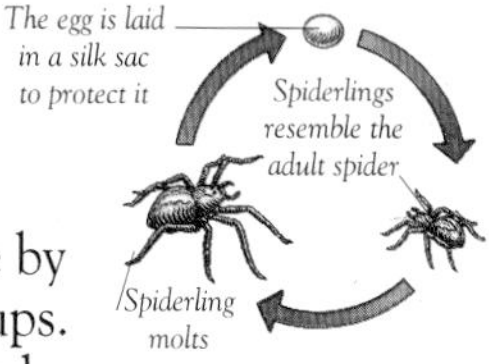

LIFE CYCLE OF A SPIDER
Arachnids such as spiders lay eggs that hatch into tiny versions of adults. They molt several times before they are mature.

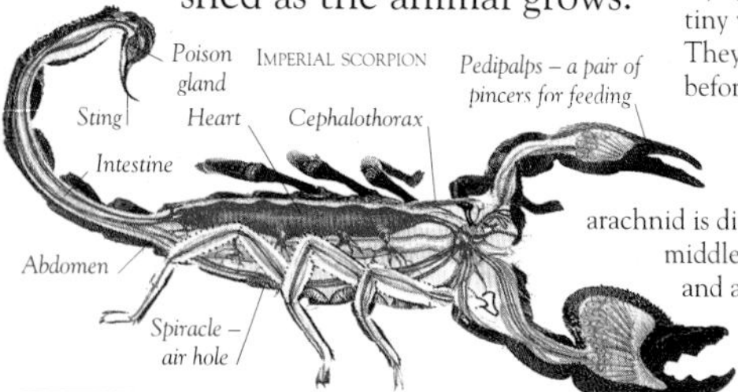

IMPERIAL SCORPION

INSIDE AN ARACHNID
The body of an arachnid is divided into a front and middle part (cephalothorax) and a rear part (abdomen). Arachnids have four pairs of walking legs.

TYPES OF ARACHNIDS

The class Arachnida includes spiders, mites, and scorpions. It contains 73,000 species, which are grouped into ten orders. Six orders are listed below.

ARACHNID	NAME OF ORDER	NUMBER OF SPECIES	ARACHNID	NAME OF ORDER	NUMBER OF SPECIES
	Scorpiones (scorpions)	2,000		Uropygi (whip scorpions)	60
	Solifugae (camel spiders)	900		Opiliones (harvestmen)	4,500
	Acari (mites and ticks)	30,000		Araneae (spiders)	40,000

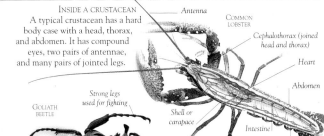

Inside a crustacean

A typical crustacean has a hard body case with a head, thorax, and abdomen. It has compound eyes, two pairs of antennae, and many pairs of jointed legs.

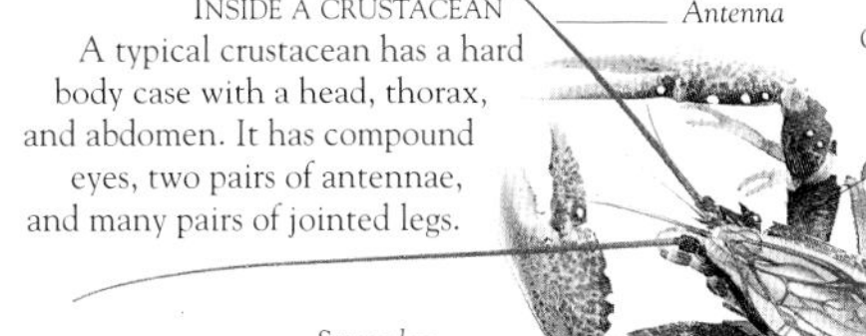

Goliath beetle

Strong legs used for fighting

Elytron

A beetle

The Goliath beetle is the world's heaviest. It weighs up to 3.5 oz (100 g). Beetles are very well armored. Their forewings are hardened, curved plates called elytra. The elytra protect the fragile hind wings that are used for flying.

Types of crustaceans

There are more than 55,000 species of crustaceans divided into eight classes. These include the four classes below.

Crustacean	Name of class	Features	Number of species
	Branchiopods (fairy shrimp, water fleas)	Small animals of freshwater and salty lakes	1, 000
	Cirripedia (barnacles)	Immobile animals with a boxlike case	1,220
	Copepods (cyclopoids and relatives)	Small animals often found in plankton	13, 000
	Malacostracans (shrimp, crabs, lobsters)	Many-legged animals, often with pincers	30, 000

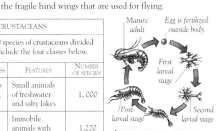

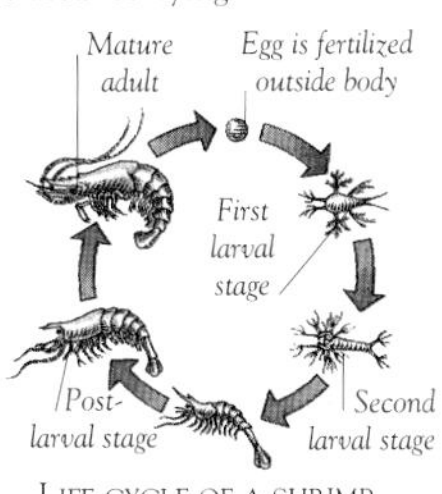

Life cycle of a shrimp

Crustaceans usually lay their eggs in water. Once hatched, the egg begins its first larval stage. After two more larval stages, there is a final post-larval stage before adulthood.

Classification

BIOLOGISTS HAVE identified and classified most species of vertebrates (animals with backbones), although it is likely that new species of fish await discovery. Invertebrates have not been so well documented and there may be many species to be identified.

Springtails
Bristletails
Diplurans
Silverfish
Mayflies
Stoneflies
Webspinners
Dragonflies
Grasshoppers, crickets
Stick and leaf insects
Grylloblattids
Earwigs
Cockroaches
Praying mantids
Termites
Lice
Thrips
Booklice
Zorapterans
Bugs
Beetles
Ants, bees, wasps
Lacewings and antlions
Scorpionflies
Stylopids
Caddisflies
Butterflies and moths
Flies
Fleas

INSECTS (Insecta) 1,000,000 species

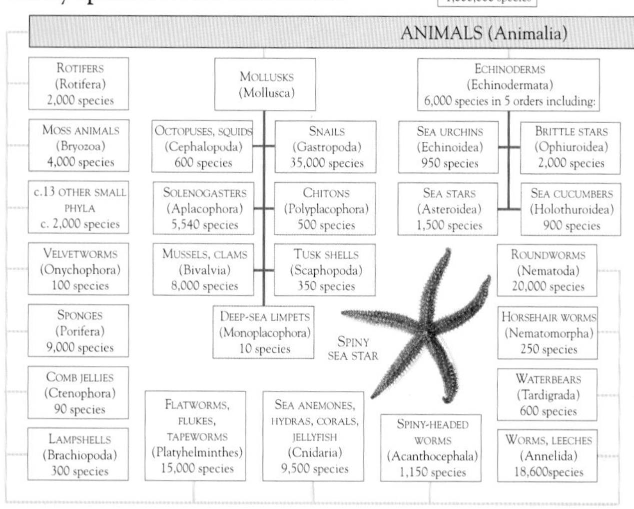

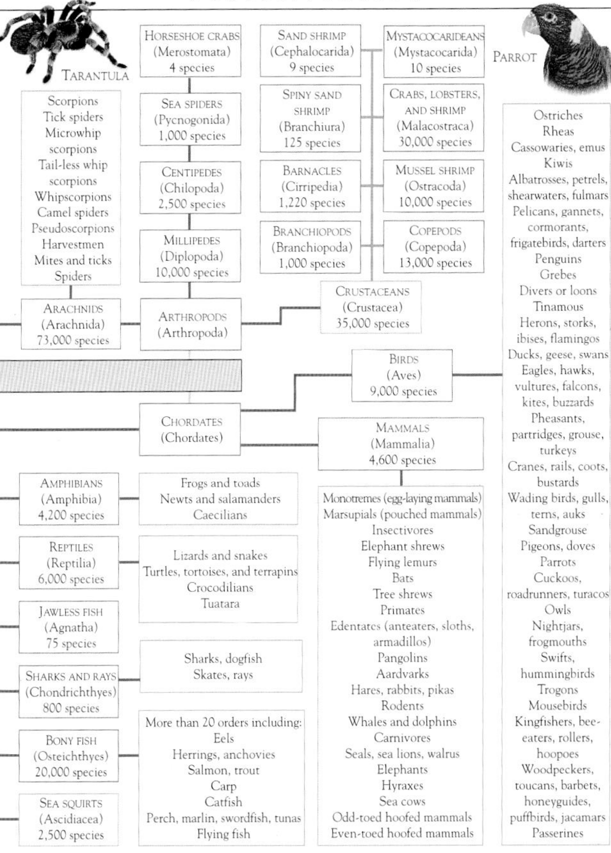
TARANTULA
Scorpions
Tick spiders
Microwhip scorpions
Tail-less whip scorpions
Whipscorpions
Camel spiders
Pseudoscorpions
Harvestmen
Mites and ticks
Spiders
ARACHNIDS (Arachnida) 73,000 species
HORSESHOE CRABS (Merostomata) 4 species
SEA SPIDERS (Pycnogonida) 1,000 species
CENTIPEDES (Chilopoda) 2,500 species
MILLIPEDES (Diplopoda) 10,000 species
ARTHROPODS (Arthropoda)
SAND SHRIMP (Cephalocarida) 9 species
SPINY SAND SHRIMP (Branchiura) 125 species
BARNACLES (Cirripedia) 1,220 species
BRANCHIOPODS (Branchiopoda) 1,000 species
MYSTACOCARIDEANS (Mystacocarida) 10 species
CRABS, LOBSTERS, AND SHRIMP (Malacostraca) 30,000 species
MUSSEL SHRIMP (Ostracoda) 10,000 species
COPEPODS (Copepoda) 13,000 species
CRUSTACEANS (Crustacea) 35,000 species
PARROT
Ostriches
Rheas
Cassowaries, emus
Kiwis
Albatrosses, petrels, shearwaters, fulmars
Pelicans, gannets, cormorants, frigatebirds, darters
Penguins
Grebes
Divers or loons
Tinamous
Herons, storks, ibises, flamingos
Ducks, geese, swans
Eagles, hawks, vultures, falcons, kites, buzzards
Pheasants, partridges, grouse, turkeys
Cranes, rails, coots, bustards
Wading birds, gulls, terns, auks
Sandgrouse
Pigeons, doves
Parrots
Cuckoos, roadrunners, turacos
Owls
Nightjars, frogmouths
Swifts, hummingbirds
Trogons
Mousebirds
Kingfishers, bee-eaters, rollers, hoopoes
Woodpeckers, toucans, barbets, honeyguides, puffbirds, jacamars
Passerines
BIRDS (Aves) 9,000 species
CHORDATES (Chordates)
MAMMALS (Mammalia) 4,600 species
Monotremes (egg-laying mammals)
Marsupials (pouched mammals)
Insectivores
Elephant shrews
Flying lemurs
Bats
Tree shrews
Primates
Edentates (anteaters, sloths, armadillos)
Pangolins
Aardvarks
Hares, rabbits, pikas
Rodents
Whales and dolphins
Carnivores
Seals, sea lions, walrus
Elephants
Hyraxes
Sea cows
Odd-toed hoofed mammals
Even-toed hoofed mammals
AMPHIBIANS (Amphibia) 4,200 species
Frogs and toads
Newts and salamanders
Caecilians
REPTILES (Reptilia) 6,000 species
Lizards and snakes
Turtles, tortoises, and terrapins
Crocodilians
Tuatara
JAWLESS FISH (Agnatha) 75 species
SHARKS AND RAYS (Chondrichthyes) 800 species
Sharks, dogfish
Skates, rays
BONY FISH (Osteichthyes) 20,000 species
More than 20 orders including:
Eels
Herrings, anchovies
Salmon, trout
Carp
Catfish
Perch, marlin, swordfish, tunas
Flying fish
SEA SQUIRTS (Ascidiacea) 2,500 species

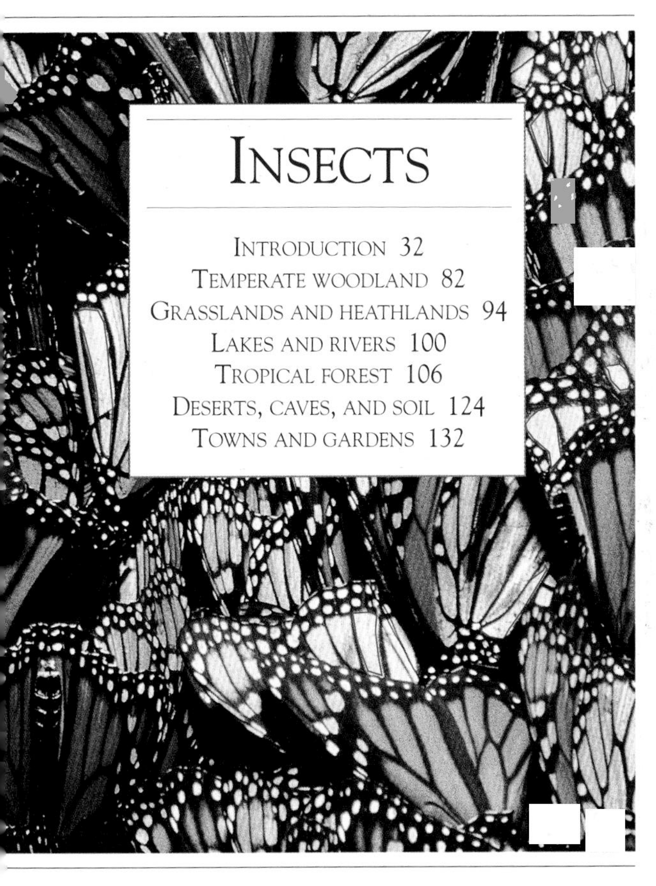

INSECTS

WHAT IS AN INSECT?

THERE ARE AT LEAST one million named insect species – they are the most abundant animals on earth. All insects have six legs, and their skeleton is on the outside of their body. This outer skeleton forms a hard, protective armor around the soft internal organs.

The antennae of insects can sense smells and vibrations in the air.

DISSECTED BEETLE

Eye

First part of thorax bears the front legs.

Jointed front leg

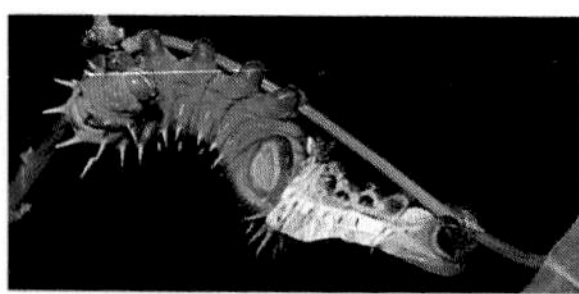

SHEDDING SKIN
An immature insect is called a nymph. As each nymph feeds and grows, it must shed its hard outer skin, which is also called an exoskeleton. When it grows too big for its skin, the skin splits, revealing a new, larger skin underneath.

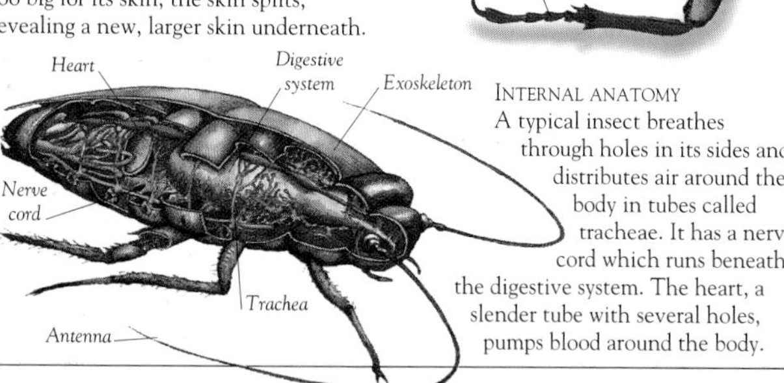

INTERNAL ANATOMY
A typical insect breathes through holes in its sides and distributes air around the body in tubes called tracheae. It has a nerve cord which runs beneath the digestive system. The heart, a slender tube with several holes, pumps blood around the body.

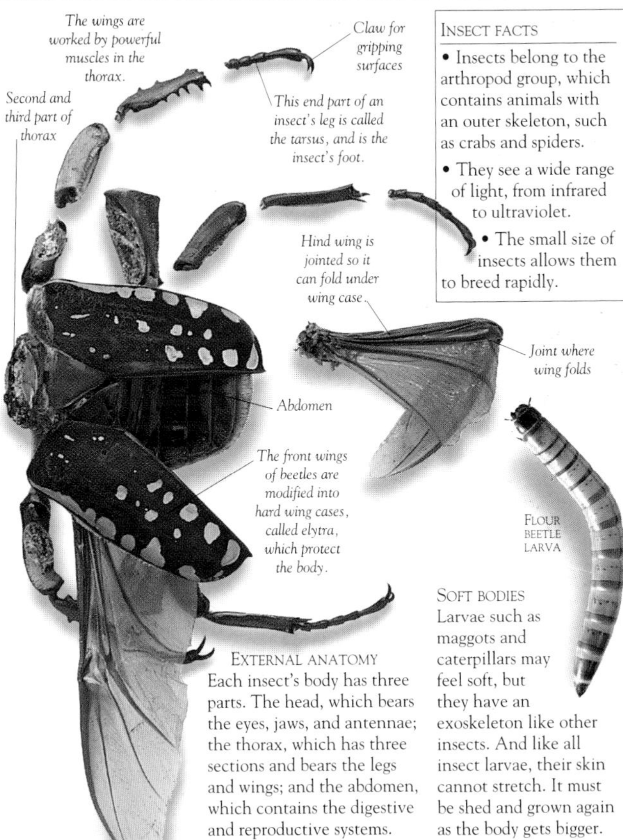

The wings are worked by powerful muscles in the thorax.
Claw for gripping surfaces
Second and third part of thorax
This end part of an insect's leg is called the tarsus, and is the insect's foot.
Hind wing is jointed so it can fold under wing case.
Joint where wing folds
Abdomen
The front wings of beetles are modified into hard wing cases, called elytra, which protect the body.
FLOUR BEETLE LARVA

INSECT FACTS

- Insects belong to the arthropod group, which contains animals with an outer skeleton, such as crabs and spiders.
- They see a wide range of light, from infrared to ultraviolet.
- The small size of insects allows them to breed rapidly.

EXTERNAL ANATOMY

Each insect's body has three parts. The head, which bears the eyes, jaws, and antennae; the thorax, which has three sections and bears the legs and wings; and the abdomen, which contains the digestive and reproductive systems.

SOFT BODIES

Larvae such as maggots and caterpillars may feel soft, but they have an exoskeleton like other insects. And like all insect larvae, their skin cannot stretch. It must be shed and grown again as the body gets bigger.

THE FIRST INSECTS

INSECTS WERE the first animals to fly. They appeared 300 million years ago – long before humans, and even before the dinosaurs. The ancient insect species are now extinct, but some were similar to modern dragonflies and cockroaches.

FLOWER FOOD
When flowering plants evolved 100 million years ago, insects gained two important new foods – pollen and nectar. Insects thrived on these foods. They pollinated the flowers, and many new species of plants and insects evolved together.

INSECT IN AMBER
Amber is the fossilized tree resin which came from pine trees over 40 million years ago. Well-preserved ancient insects are sometimes found in amber. This bee is in copal, which is similar to amber but not as old.

FIRST INSECT FACTS

- The oldest known fossil insect is a springtail that lived 400 million years ago.
- Some of the earliest insects seem to have had three pairs of wings.
- The oldest known butterfly or moth is known from England 190 million years ago.

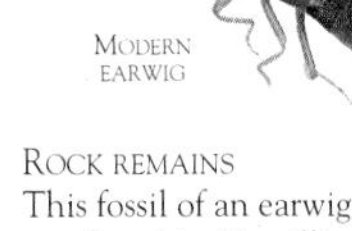

MODERN EARWIG

ROCK REMAINS
This fossil of an earwig was found in 35-million-year-old lake sediment in Colorado. The fossil shows how similar in shape ancient earwigs were to modern ones.

Fossil earwig

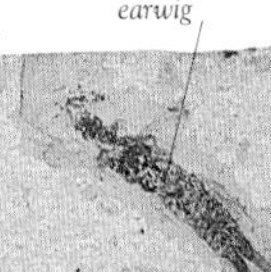

FOSSIL DRAGONFLY
Dragonflies were one of the first types of insect. Fossils show that they have not changed very much in appearance over millions of years. Some ancient dragonflies were very large and may have had wing-spans of over 2 ft (60 cm). This dragonfly fossil, found in southern England, is of a small species. The intricate wing veins can be seen clearly.

MODERN DRAGONFLY
One of the largest present-day dragonflies is this species from Borneo, with a wingspan of 6¼ in (16 cm). Although the larvae of modern dragonflies live in water, we cannot be sure that this was true of prehistoric dragonflies.

AGILE FLIERS
Modern dragonflies are fast, agile fliers, and ancient dragonflies were probably the same. A prehistoric flying reptile would have had greater trouble catching a dragonfly than this fanciful engraving suggests.

TYPES OF INSECT

WE DO NOT KNOW exactly how many species, or types, of insect there are, since scientists constantly discover new insects. There are about one million different named species. Each belongs to one of about 28 groups, or orders, which are defined according to body structure and larval development.

Beetles, wasps, bees, and ants

About 350,000 species of beetles are described – they are the largest order of insects. Wasps, bees, and ants form the second largest order of insects, made up of about 125,000 species. The common feature in this order is a narrow "waist."

Jaws

STAG BEETLE

Hard wing cases meet in midline.

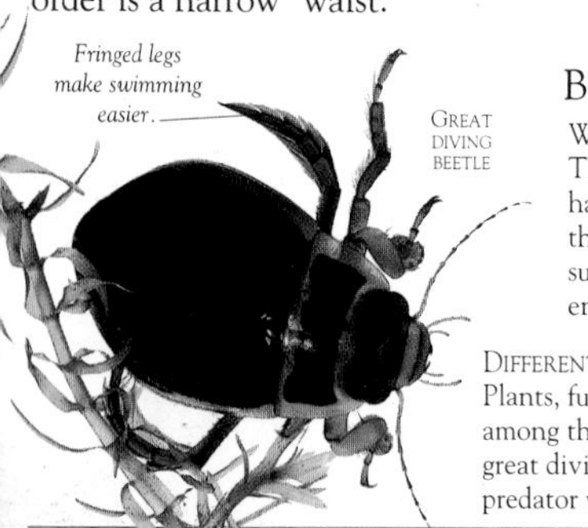
Fringed legs make swimming easier.
GREAT DIVING BEETLE

BEETLES

WINGS AND JAWS

The front pair of wings in beetles is hardened and forms a strong shield over the folded hind wings. Some beetles, such as stag beetles, have greatly enlarged jaws that look like horns.

DIFFERENT FOODS

Plants, fungi, insects, and dead animals are among the wide variety of beetle foods. The great diving beetle lives in ponds. It is a fierce predator which hunts tadpoles and small fish.

Ants, wasps, and bees

Wasps

Adult wasps have a narrow "waist" and two pairs of transparent wings. The larvae look like grubs or caterpillars. Female wasps have an egg-laying tube that is often modified to form a sting.

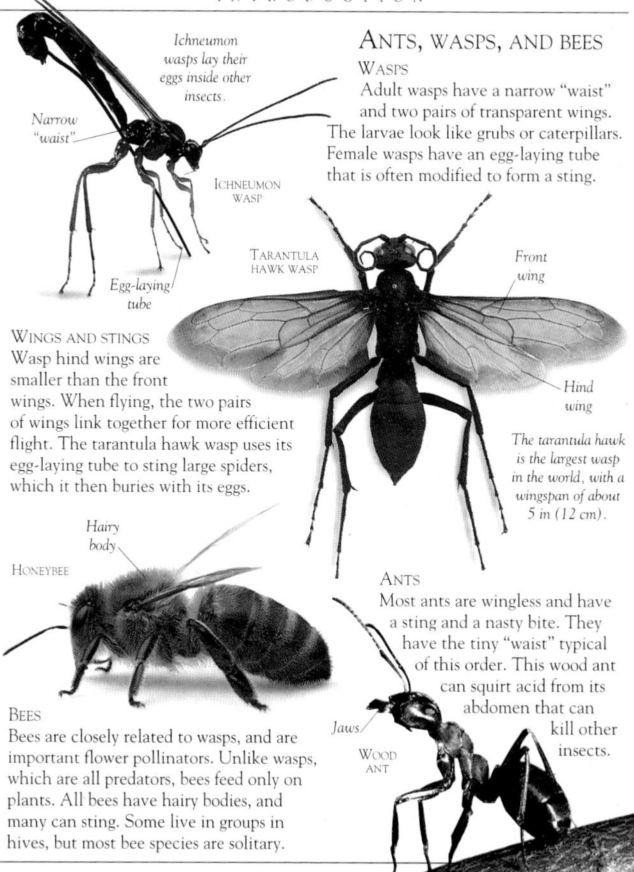

Ichneumon wasps lay their eggs inside other insects.

The tarantula hawk is the largest wasp in the world, with a wingspan of about 5 in (12 cm).

Wings and stings

Wasp hind wings are smaller than the front wings. When flying, the two pairs of wings link together for more efficient flight. The tarantula hawk wasp uses its egg-laying tube to sting large spiders, which it then buries with its eggs.

Ants

Most ants are wingless and have a sting and a nasty bite. They have the tiny "waist" typical of this order. This wood ant can squirt acid from its abdomen that can kill other insects.

Bees

Bees are closely related to wasps, and are important flower pollinators. Unlike wasps, which are all predators, bees feed only on plants. All bees have hairy bodies, and many can sting. Some live in groups in hives, but most bee species are solitary.

Butterflies, moths, and flies

Two common insect orders are the two-winged flies and the butterflies and moths. Flies are distinctive because their second pair of wings is converted into balancing organs that look like drumsticks. Their young stages are maggots. Butterflies and moths have a coiled feeding tube, and their wings are covered in minute, flattened scales. Butterfly and moth larvae are called caterpillars.

BUTTERFLIES AND MOTHS

CATERPILLARS

Although caterpillars' bodies are soft, they have an exoskeleton like other insects. Caterpillars grow at a very fast rate. They feed on leaves and have sharp jaws for slicing vegetation.

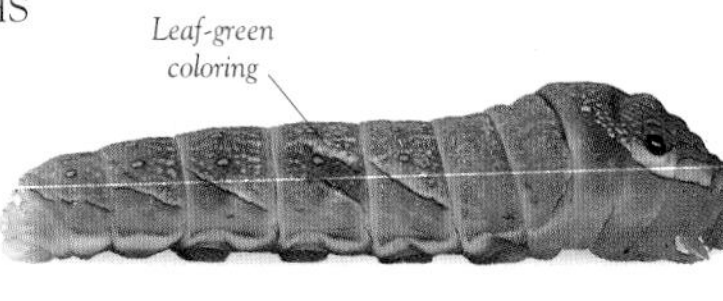

POLYPHEMUS MOTH

MOTHS

There are 150,000 species of moth. Most moth species fly only at night. They are usually dull in color and they often have feathery antennae. There are also many day-flying species, and some of these are brightly colored.

BUTTERFLIES

There are 15,000 species of butterfly. Most butterflies fly by day, have club-tipped antennae, and are brightly colored. The scales that cover moths and butterflies sometimes produce colors by iridescence, which is the effect of sunlight shining on them to produce a display of many different colors.

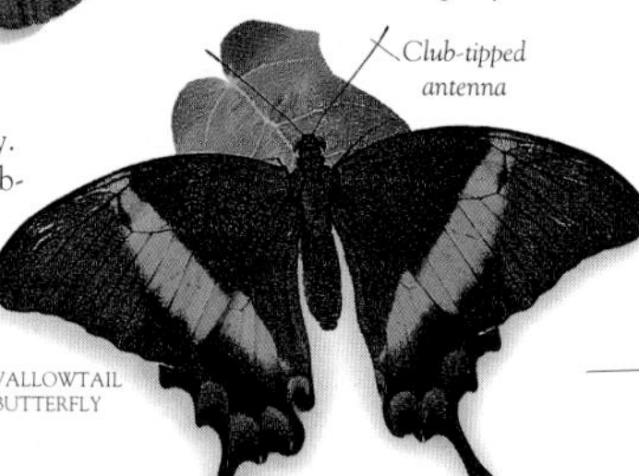

SWALLOWTAIL BUTTERFLY

FLIES

CRANE-FLY

Crane-flies live successfully all over the world. The larvae of some species of crane-fly are known as "leather-jackets," because their skin is so tough.

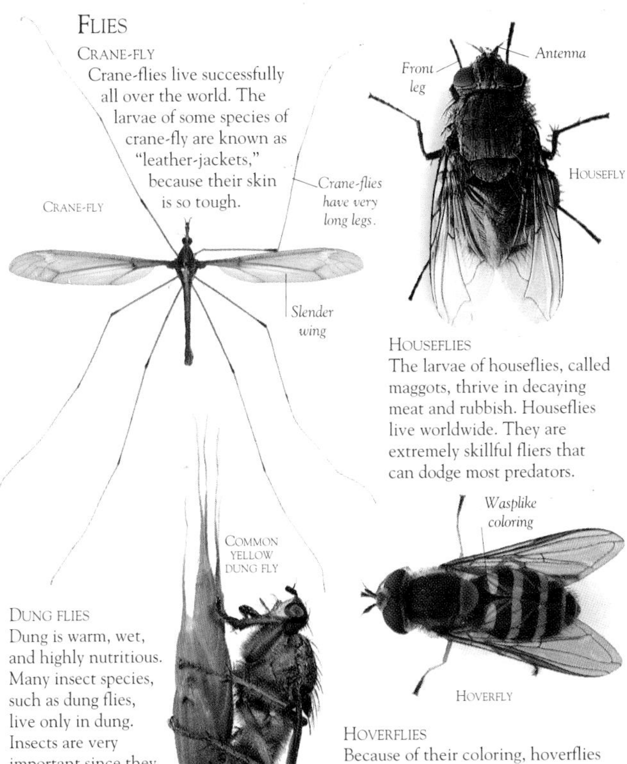

HOUSEFLIES

The larvae of houseflies, called maggots, thrive in decaying meat and rubbish. Houseflies live worldwide. They are extremely skillful fliers that can dodge most predators.

DUNG FLIES

Dung is warm, wet, and highly nutritious. Many insect species, such as dung flies, live only in dung. Insects are very important since they help clear up the droppings of much larger animals.

HOVERFLIES

Because of their coloring, hoverflies are often mistaken for wasps. They are fantastic fliers, able to hover, and to dart from place to place at great speed.

Bugs and other types

There are about 67,500 species of bug, the fifth-largest order of insects. Bugs have a feeding tube folded back between the legs, and most of them eat plant food. The other orders of insects contain fewer species. Some of these orders are well known, such as fleas, cockroaches, dragonflies, and locusts.

BUGS

FEEDING TUBES

The mandibles (jaws) found in most insects are modified into needlelike tubes in bugs. The bug pierces food with the feeding tube and then sucks up juices.

PLANT BUG

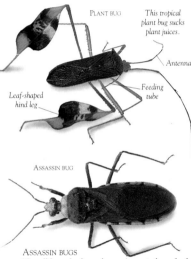

This tropical plant bug sucks plant juices.

Antenna

Feeding tube

Leaf-shaped hind leg

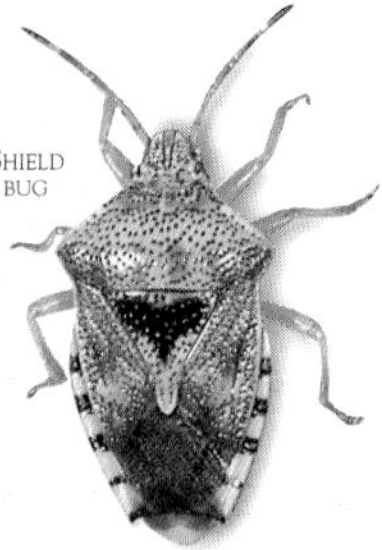

SHIELD BUG

ASSASSIN BUG

SHIELD BUGS

Bugs have two pairs of wings. The front wings are quite hard, although not as hard as those of beetles. Shield bugs are so called because when their wings are closed, they look like colorful shields.

ASSASSIN BUGS

Not all bugs feed on plants. Assassin bugs feed on other insects. They stab prey with their feeding tube and then suck out the victim's juices. Some South American assassin bugs feed on the blood of humans and transmit diseases.

OTHER INSECT ORDERS

GRASSHOPPERS

The desert locust is a member of the grasshopper order. These insects eat plants and have powerful back legs for leaping.

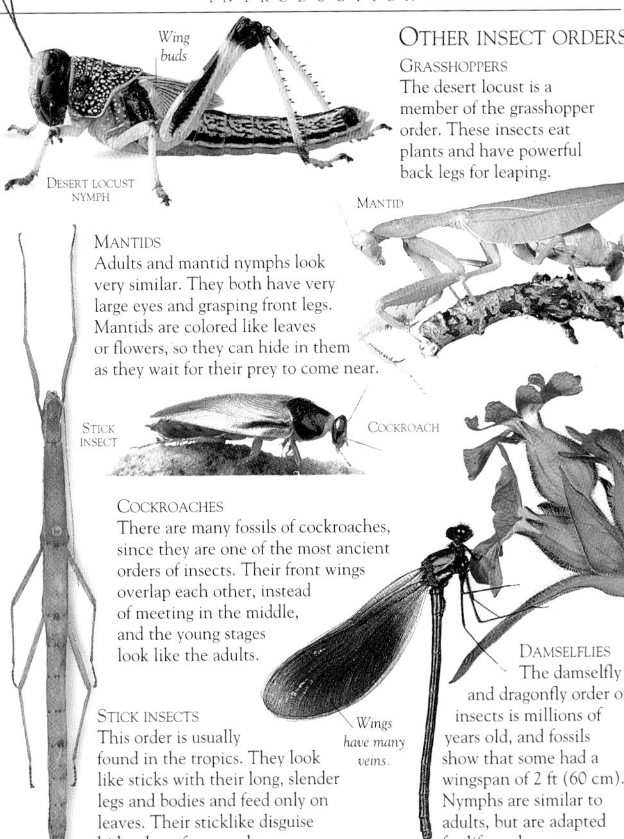

MANTIDS

Adults and mantid nymphs look very similar. They both have very large eyes and grasping front legs. Mantids are colored like leaves or flowers, so they can hide in them as they wait for their prey to come near.

COCKROACHES

There are many fossils of cockroaches, since they are one of the most ancient orders of insects. Their front wings overlap each other, instead of meeting in the middle, and the young stages look like the adults.

STICK INSECTS

This order is usually found in the tropics. They look like sticks with their long, slender legs and bodies and feed only on leaves. Their sticklike disguise hides them from predators.

DAMSELFLIES

The damselfly and dragonfly order of insects is millions of years old, and fossils show that some had a wingspan of 2 ft (60 cm). Nymphs are similar to adults, but are adapted for life underwater.

METAMORPHOSIS

INSECTS GO THROUGH several stages of growth before they become adults. This growing process is called metamorphosis. There are two types of metamorphosis: complete and incomplete. Complete metamorphosis has four growth stages – egg, larva, pupa, and adult. Incomplete metamorphosis involves three stages – egg, nymph, and adult.

Incomplete metamorphosis

This growing process is a gradual transformation. The insects hatch from their eggs looking like miniature adults. These young insects are called nymphs. As they grow, they shed their skin several times before they reach the adult stage.

1 DAMSELFLY NYMPH
A damselfly nymph lives underwater. Paddle-like plates on its tail help it swim and breathe. It sheds its skin several times as it grows toward adulthood.

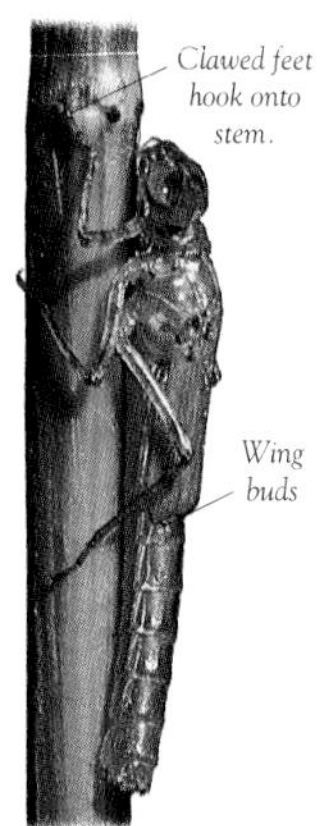
Clawed feet hook onto stem.
Wing buds

2 HOLDING ON
When the nymph is ready to change into an adult it crawls out of the water up a plant stem.

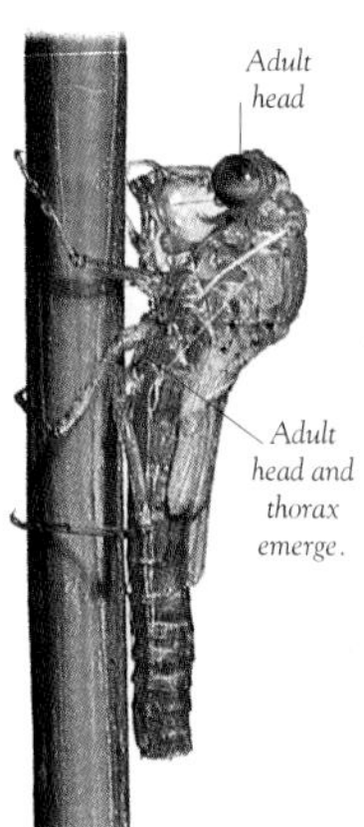
Adult head
Adult head and thorax emerge.

3 BREAKING OUT
The skin along the back splits open and the adult head and thorax start to emerge.

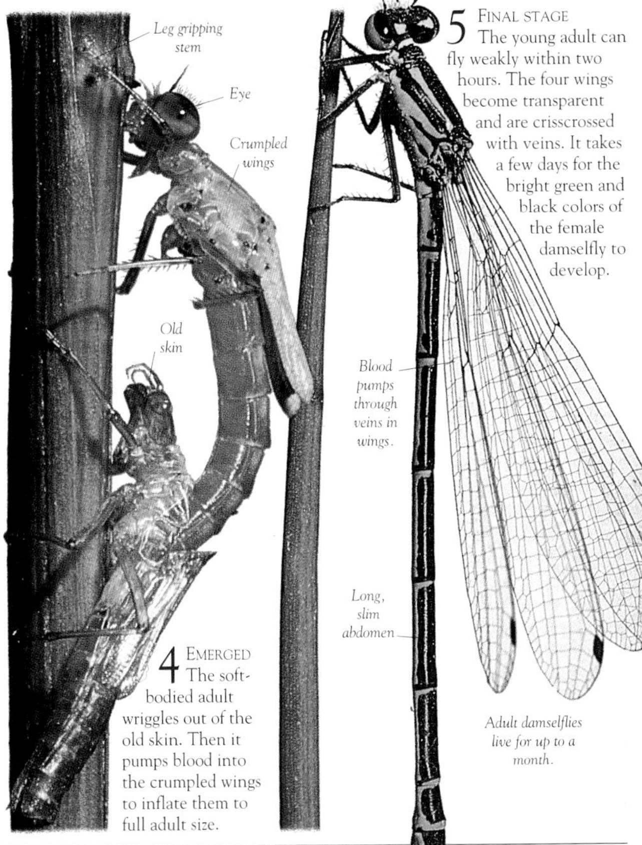

4 EMERGED The soft-bodied adult wriggles out of the old skin. Then it pumps blood into the crumpled wings to inflate them to full adult size.

5 FINAL STAGE The young adult can fly weakly within two hours. The four wings become transparent and are crisscrossed with veins. It takes a few days for the bright green and black colors of the female damselfly to develop.

Adult damselflies live for up to a month.

Complete metamorphosis

The four growth stages in a complete metamorphosis are egg, larva, pupa, and adult. The larva bears no resemblance to the adult it will become. During the pupa stage the larva makes the amazing transformation into an adult. Insects such as wasps, butterflies, beetles, and flies undergo complete metamorphosis.

1 LAYING EGGS Butterflies lay eggs near leaves that caterpillars can eat when they hatch. Newly hatched caterpillars are too small to walk far to feed.

2 THE FIRST MEAL When a caterpillar emerges, the first meal it eats is usually its own eggshell. The eggshell provides the caterpillar with valuable nutrients before it begins its diet of leaves.

A caterpillar can increase its body weight by about 100 times in a few weeks.

3 GROWING The caterpillar chews up leaves and grows much bigger, shedding its skin several times. This growth prepares the caterpillar for the pupal stage of its life.

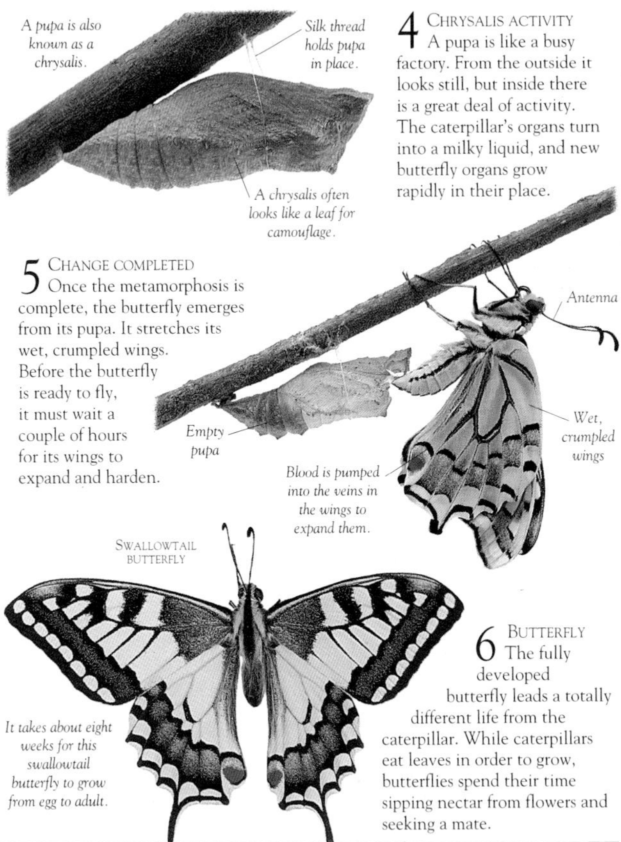

A pupa is also known as a chrysalis.
Silk thread holds pupa in place.
A chrysalis often looks like a leaf for camouflage.
Antenna
Empty pupa
Wet, crumpled wings
Blood is pumped into the veins in the wings to expand them.
SWALLOWTAIL BUTTERFLY
It takes about eight weeks for this swallowtail butterfly to grow from egg to adult.

4 CHRYSALIS ACTIVITY
A pupa is like a busy factory. From the outside it looks still, but inside there is a great deal of activity. The caterpillar's organs turn into a milky liquid, and new butterfly organs grow rapidly in their place.

5 CHANGE COMPLETED
Once the metamorphosis is complete, the butterfly emerges from its pupa. It stretches its wet, crumpled wings. Before the butterfly is ready to fly, it must wait a couple of hours for its wings to expand and harden.

6 BUTTERFLY
The fully developed butterfly leads a totally different life from the caterpillar. While caterpillars eat leaves in order to grow, butterflies spend their time sipping nectar from flowers and seeking a mate.

How insects move

INSECTS MOVE using muscles which are attached to the inner surfaces of their hard outer skeleton. Many insects walk, but some larvae have no legs and have to crawl. Some insects swim, others jump, but most adult insects can fly and in this way they may travel long distances.

Legs

Insects use their legs for walking, running, jumping, and swimming. Many insects have legs modified for a number of other purposes. These include catching prey, holding a female when mating, producing songs, digging, fighting, and camouflage.

LEGS FOR SWIMMING
The water boatman has long, oar-shaped back legs, allowing the insect to "row" rapidly through water. The legs have flattened ends and a fringe of thick hairs. The front legs are short to grasp prey on the water surface.

LEGS FACTS

- Fairy flies, which live as parasites on the eggs of water insects, can "fly" underwater.
- Many butterflies walk on four legs; the front pair are used for tasting.
- The legless larvae of some parasitic wasps hitch a ride on a passing ant in order to enter an ant's nest.

1 PREPARING TO JUMP
The back legs of locusts are swollen and packed with strong muscles for jumping. Before leaping, a locust holds its back legs tightly under its body, near its center of gravity. This is the best position for the legs to propel the insect high into the air.

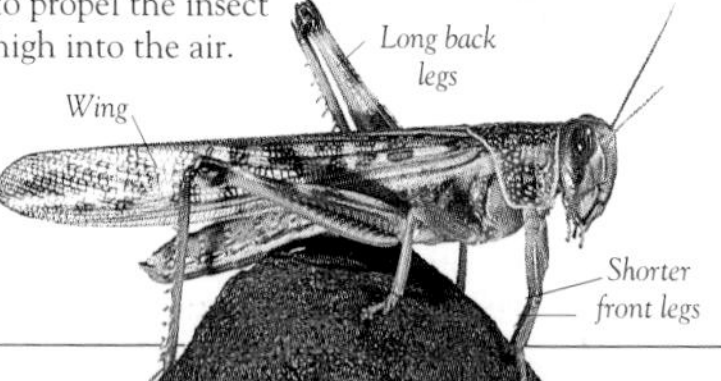

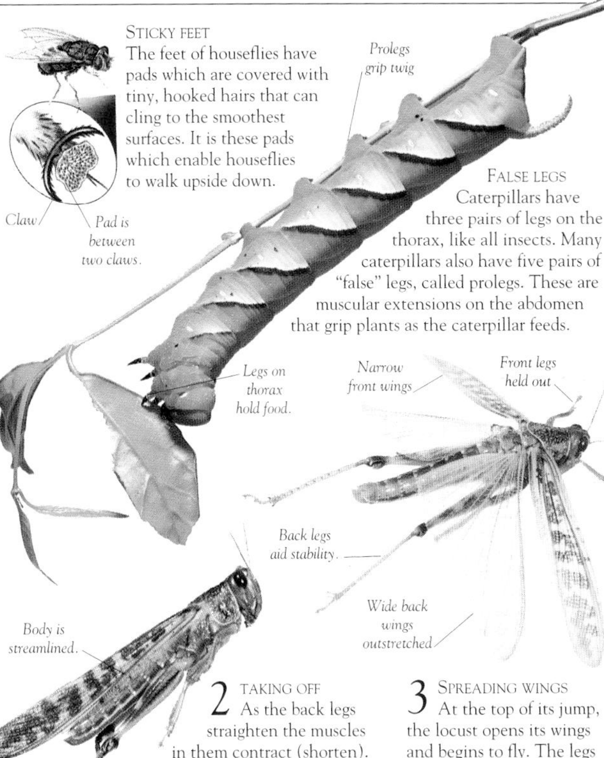

Claw
Pad is between two claws.
Prolegs grip twig
Legs on thorax hold food.
Narrow front wings
Front legs held out
Back legs aid stability.
Wide back wings outstretched
Body is streamlined.

STICKY FEET

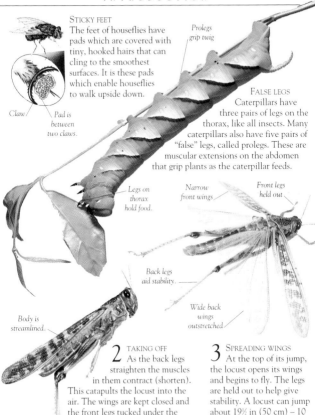

The feet of houseflies have pads which are covered with tiny, hooked hairs that can cling to the smoothest surfaces. It is these pads which enable houseflies to walk upside down.

FALSE LEGS

Caterpillars have three pairs of legs on the thorax, like all insects. Many caterpillars also have five pairs of "false" legs, called prolegs. These are muscular extensions on the abdomen that grip plants as the caterpillar feeds.

2 TAKING OFF

As the back legs straighten the muscles in them contract (shorten). This catapults the locust into the air. The wings are kept closed and the front legs tucked under the body, so the insect is streamlined.

3 SPREADING WINGS

At the top of its jump, the locust opens its wings and begins to fly. The legs are held out to help give stability. A locust can jump about 19½ in (50 cm) – 10 times its own body length.

Wings and scales

Insect wings are a wide variety of shapes and sizes. They are used not just for flying, but also for attracting a mate or hiding from predators. Most insects have two pairs of wings, each with a network of veins to give strength. Flies have only one pair of wings – the second pair is modified into small balancing organs called halteres. Small insects have few wing veins since their wings are so tiny.

EXPERT FLIERS

Dragonflies are among the most accomplished fliers in the insect world. They can hover, fly fast or slow, change direction rapidly, and even fly backward. As they maneuver, their two pairs of wings beat independently of each other.

WING FACTS

- The scales of butterflies and moths contain waste products from the pupal stage.
- There is a hearing organ in one of the wing veins of green lacewings for hearing the shrieks of bats.
- Many species of island insects are wingless because of the risk of being blown out to sea.

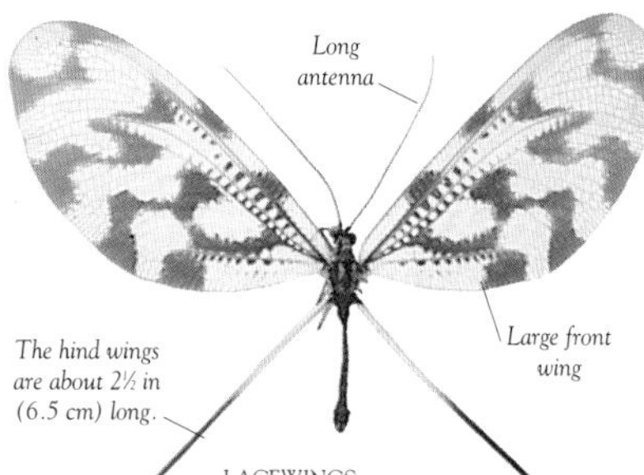

LACEWINGS

The hind wings of ribbon-tail lacewings are modified into long graceful streamers. Scientists are not sure what these are for, but they may act as stabilizers in flight, or even divert predators from attacking the lacewing's body. The lacewing's mottled patterns probably help to conceal it in the dry, sandy places where it lives.

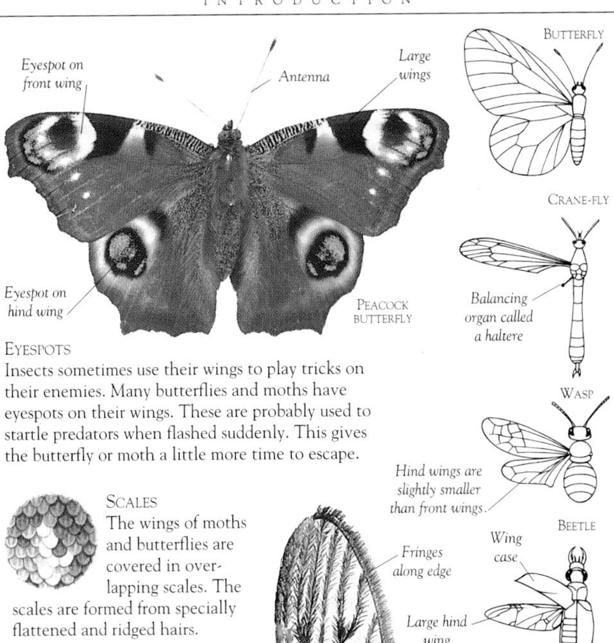

EYESPOTS

Insects sometimes use their wings to play tricks on their enemies. Many butterflies and moths have eyespots on their wings. These are probably used to startle predators when flashed suddenly. This gives the butterfly or moth a little more time to escape.

SCALES

The wings of moths and butterflies are covered in overlapping scales. The scales are formed from specially flattened and ridged hairs.

FRINGED WINGS

Tiny insects have difficulty in flying since air is very dense for them. To increase the size of their wings and so improve lift, they often have fringes of hairs around the edges of the wings.

DIFFERENT WINGS

Most butterflies have two pairs of large wings. Flies have only one pair of wings. The wings of wasps are transparent. Beetles' second pair of large wings is folded away under the hardened first pair, or wing cases.

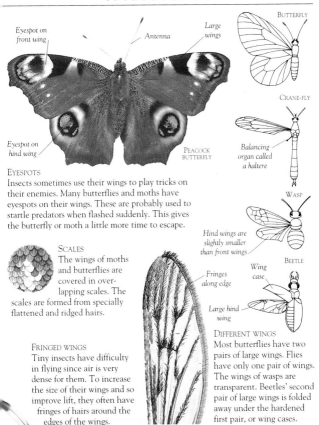

Flight

The ability to fly is one of the main reasons insects have survived for millions of years, and continue to flourish. Flight helps insects escape from danger. It also makes it easier to find food and new places to live. Sometimes insects fly thousands of miles to reach fresh food or warmer weather.

Flying groups

This African grasshopper has broad hind wings which allow it to glide for long distances. Locusts are a type of grasshopper that fly in huge groups when they need new food. Sometimes as many as 100 million locusts fly together for hundreds of miles.

Warming up

An insect's flight muscles must be warm before the wings can be moved fast enough for flight. On cool mornings, insects like this shield bug shiver, vibrating their wings to warm themselves up.

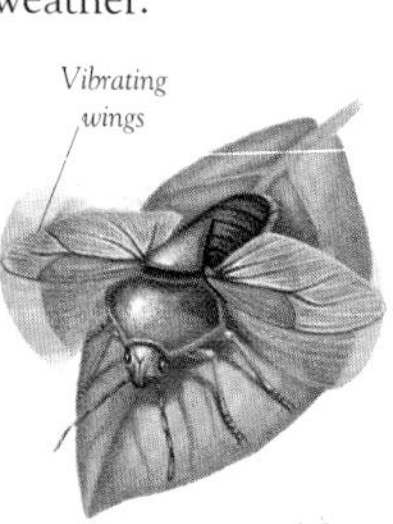

1 Preparing to fly

This cockchafer beetle prepares for flight by climbing to the top of a plant and facing into the wind. It may open and shut its elytra (wing cases) several times while warming up.

2 Opening the wings

The hardened elytra, which protect the fragile hind wings, begin to open. The antennae are spread so the beetle can monitor the wind direction.

ACROBATS OF THE AIR

Hoverflies are capable of incredible acrobatics in the air. They can move like a helicopter – forward, backward, sideways, and directly upward or downward. They can also hover, a flight maneuver that very few insects are capable of.

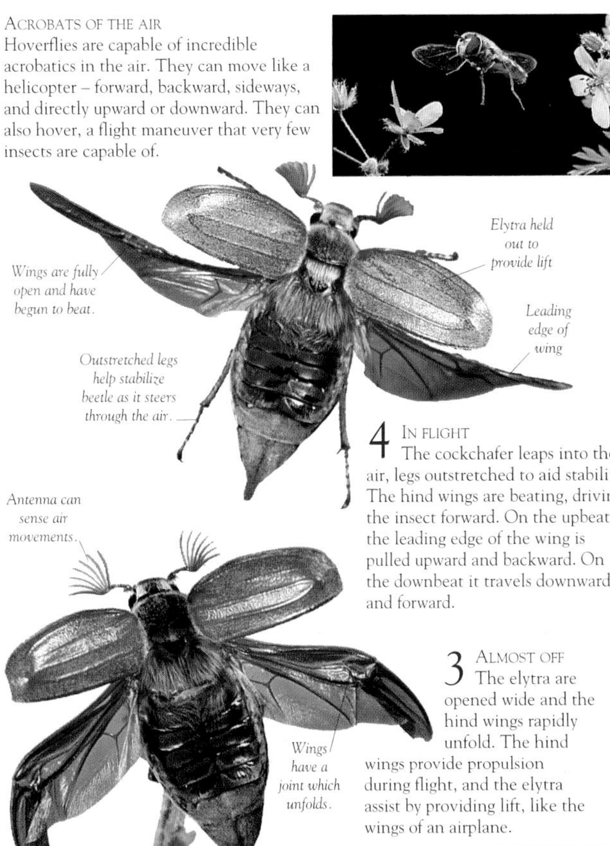

Wings are fully open and have begun to beat.
Elytra held out to provide lift
Leading edge of wing
Outstretched legs help stabilize beetle as it steers through the air.
Antenna can sense air movements.
Wings have a joint which unfolds.

4 IN FLIGHT The cockchafer leaps into the air, legs outstretched to aid stability. The hind wings are beating, driving the insect forward. On the upbeat, the leading edge of the wing is pulled upward and backward. On the downbeat it travels downward and forward.

3 ALMOST OFF The elytra are opened wide and the hind wings rapidly unfold. The hind wings provide propulsion during flight, and the elytra assist by providing lift, like the wings of an airplane.

Insect senses

INSECTS NEED to be fully aware of the world around them in order to survive. Although insects are tiny, some have keener senses than many larger animals. They can see colors and hear sounds that are undetectable to humans, as well as being able to detect smells from many miles away.

Sight

There are two types of insect eyes – simple and compound. Simple eyes can probably detect only light and shade. Compound eyes have hundreds of lenses, giving their owner excellent vision.

HEAD OF COMMON DARTER DRAGONFLY

SIMPLE EYES

Caterpillars never need to look far for their plant food – they are constantly surrounded by it. Because of this, they do not need sharp eyesight. They can manage perfectly well with a group of simple eyes.

Simple eyes

GOOD VISION

The eyes of dragonflies take up most of their head. This allows them to see what's in front, above, below, and behind them all at the same time. Dragonflies use their excellent sight and agile flight to catch prey.

COMMON DARTER DRAGONFLY

EYE CONSTRUCTION
Compound eyes are made up of many individual facets, called ommatidia. Each ommatidium has a lens at the top, with a second, conical-shaped lens underneath. The more ommatidia there are, the more sensitive is the eye.

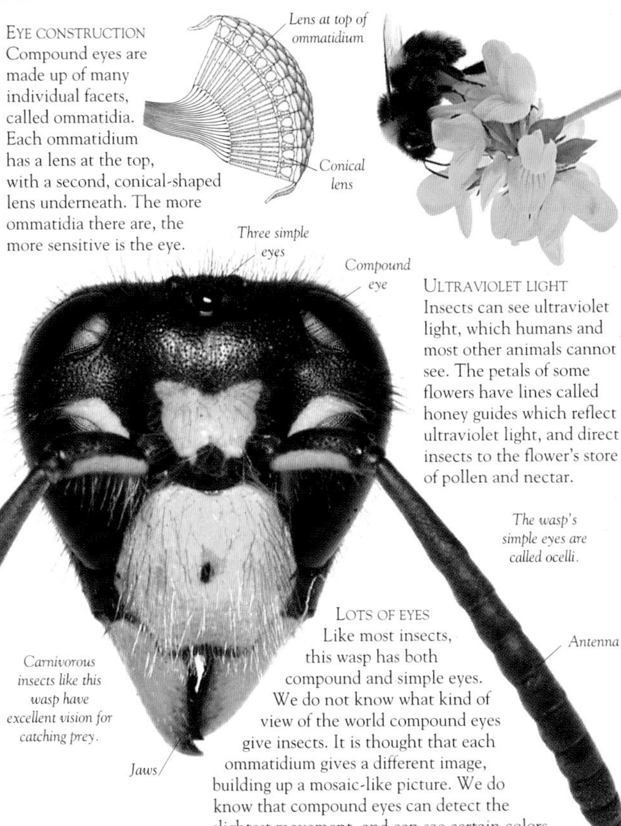

ULTRAVIOLET LIGHT
Insects can see ultraviolet light, which humans and most other animals cannot see. The petals of some flowers have lines called honey guides which reflect ultraviolet light, and direct insects to the flower's store of pollen and nectar.

The wasp's simple eyes are called ocelli.

LOTS OF EYES
Like most insects, this wasp has both compound and simple eyes. We do not know what kind of view of the world compound eyes give insects. It is thought that each ommatidium gives a different image, building up a mosaic-like picture. We do know that compound eyes can detect the slightest movement, and can see certain colors.

Carnivorous insects like this wasp have excellent vision for catching prey.

Smelling, hearing, and touching

The bodies of insects are covered in short hairs which are connected to the nervous system. These hairs can feel, or "hear," vibrations in the air due to either sound or movement. Some hairs are modified to detect smells and flavors. Sensory hairs are often found on the antennae, but also occur on the feet and mouthparts.

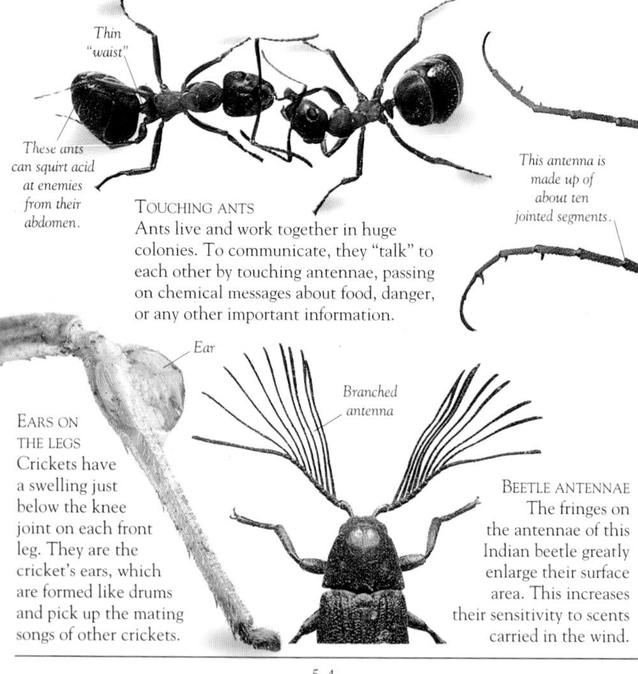

Thin "waist"
These ants can squirt acid at enemies from their abdomen.
This antenna is made up of about ten jointed segments.
Ear
Branched antenna

TOUCHING ANTS
Ants live and work together in huge colonies. To communicate, they "talk" to each other by touching antennae, passing on chemical messages about food, danger, or any other important information.

EARS ON THE LEGS
Crickets have a swelling just below the knee joint on each front leg. They are the cricket's ears, which are formed like drums and pick up the mating songs of other crickets.

BEETLE ANTENNAE
The fringes on the antennae of this Indian beetle greatly enlarge their surface area. This increases their sensitivity to scents carried in the wind.

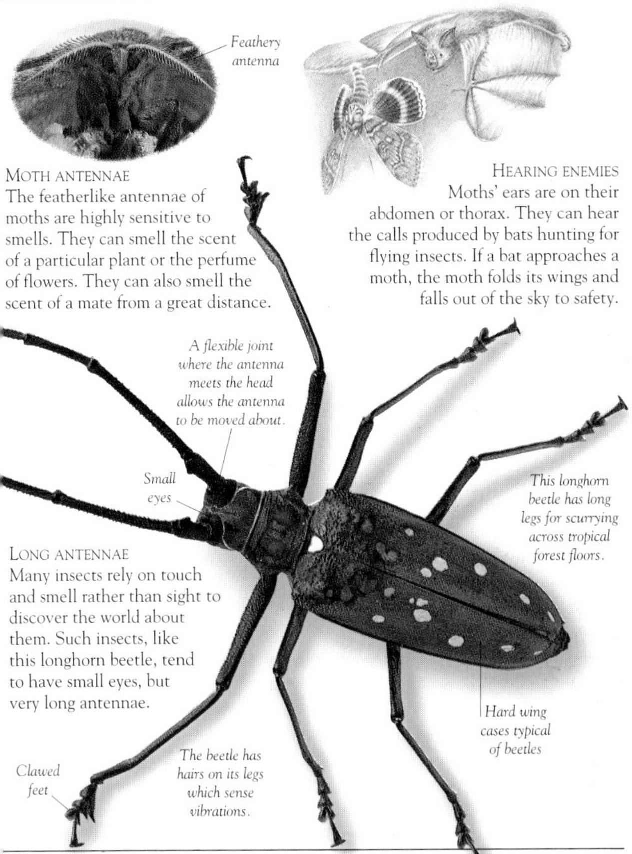

Feathery antenna
A flexible joint where the antenna meets the head allows the antenna to be moved about.
Small eyes
This longhorn beetle has long legs for scurrying across tropical forest floors.
Hard wing cases typical of beetles
The beetle has hairs on its legs which sense vibrations.
Clawed feet

MOTH ANTENNAE
The featherlike antennae of moths are highly sensitive to smells. They can smell the scent of a particular plant or the perfume of flowers. They can also smell the scent of a mate from a great distance.

HEARING ENEMIES
Moths' ears are on their abdomen or thorax. They can hear the calls produced by bats hunting for flying insects. If a bat approaches a moth, the moth folds its wings and falls out of the sky to safety.

LONG ANTENNAE
Many insects rely on touch and smell rather than sight to discover the world about them. Such insects, like this longhorn beetle, tend to have small eyes, but very long antennae.

HOW INSECTS FEED

INSECTS HAVE complex mouthparts. The insects that chew their food have a pair of strong jaws for chopping, a smaller pair of jaws for holding food, and two pairs of sensory organs, called palps, for tasting. Some insects drink only liquid food and have special tubular mouthparts like a straw.

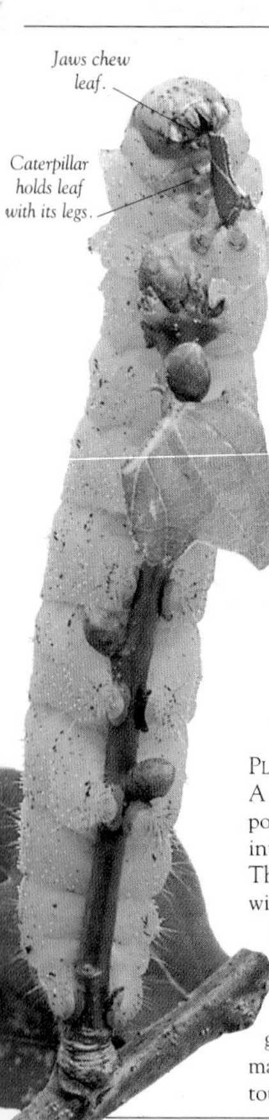
Jaws chew leaf.
Caterpillar holds leaf with its legs.

Chewing

Predatory, chewing insects need sharp, pointed jaws for stabbing, holding, and chopping up their struggling prey. Insects that chew plants have blunter jaws for grinding their food.

PLANT CHEWER
A caterpillar needs powerful jaws to bite into plant material. Their jaws are armed with teeth that overlap when they close. Some caterpillars' jaws are modified into grinding plates for mashing up the toughest leaves.

THRUSTING JAWS
Dragonfly larvae have pincers at the end of a hinged plate folded under the head. When catching prey, the plate unfolds, shoots forward, and the pincers grab the prey. Toothed jaws in the head reduce the victim to mincemeat.

BULLDOG ANT

Ants have many different jaw shapes, reflecting the variety of food they eat. Harvester ants have broad, toothless jaws for crushing seeds. Some predatory ants have long, pointed jaws for killing prey; others have simple jaws for feeding on soft-bodied insects and honeydew. This formidable bulldog ant has very large, spiky jaws for chopping up other insects.

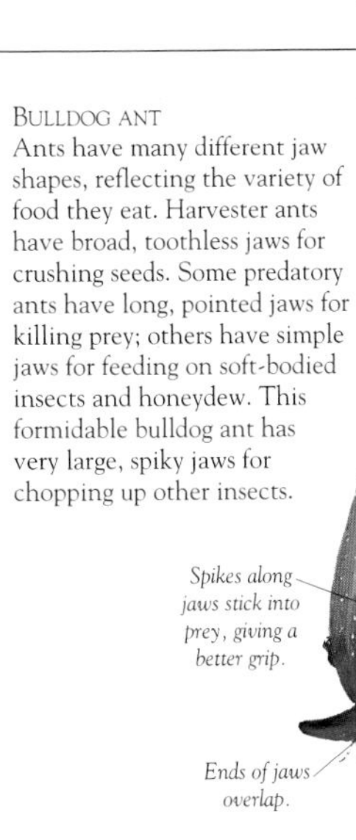
Spikes along jaws stick into prey, giving a better grip.
Ends of jaws overlap.

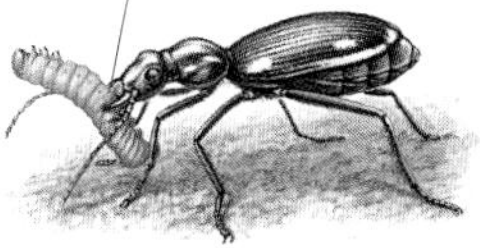

Jaws cut up caterpillar.

CHOPPING JAWS

The massive jaws of ground beetles act like a knife and fork to chop up worms, slugs, and caterpillars. A smaller pair of jaws is used to shovel the dismembered prey into its mouth.

Mantis uses its jaws to cut up a fly.
Spiny front legs hold the fly.

STRONG GRIP

The praying mantis holds its prey in a viselike grip with its spiny front legs. The strong, sharp jaws of the mantis easily slice through the prey's body, and the mantis devours the meal within a few minutes.

Drinking

For many insects, the main way of feeding is by drinking. The most nutritious foods to drink are nectar and blood. Nectar is rich in sugar, and blood is packed with proteins. Some insects drink by sucking through strawlike mouthparts. Others have spongelike mouthparts with which they mop up liquids.

HAWK MOTH
Butterflies and moths have a long, tonguelike tube called a proboscis through which they drink. Darwin's hawk moth has an extremely long proboscis for reaching the nectar in an extra-long flower.

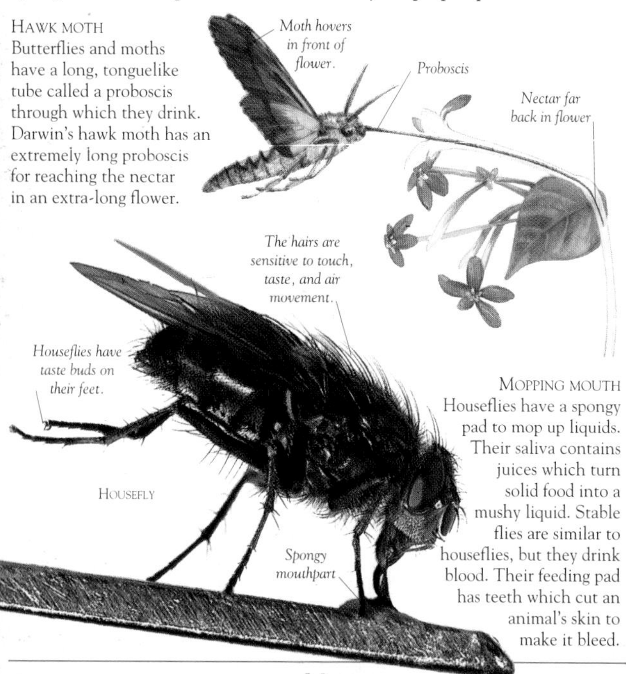

Moth hovers in front of flower.
Proboscis
Nectar far back in flower
The hairs are sensitive to touch, taste, and air movement.
Houseflies have taste buds on their feet.
HOUSEFLY
Spongy mouthpart

MOPPING MOUTH
Houseflies have a spongy pad to mop up liquids. Their saliva contains juices which turn solid food into a mushy liquid. Stable flies are similar to houseflies, but they drink blood. Their feeding pad has teeth which cut an animal's skin to make it bleed.

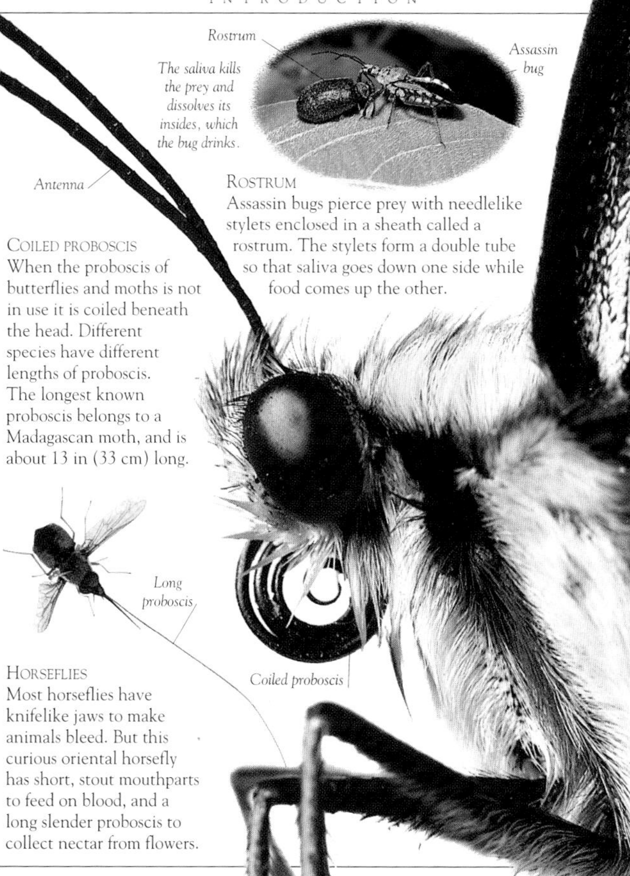

The saliva kills the prey and dissolves its insides, which the bug drinks.

ROSTRUM
Assassin bugs pierce prey with needlelike stylets enclosed in a sheath called a rostrum. The stylets form a double tube so that saliva goes down one side while food comes up the other.

COILED PROBOSCIS
When the proboscis of butterflies and moths is not in use it is coiled beneath the head. Different species have different lengths of proboscis. The longest known proboscis belongs to a Madagascan moth, and is about 13 in (33 cm) long.

HORSEFLIES
Most horseflies have knifelike jaws to make animals bleed. But this curious oriental horsefly has short, stout mouthparts to feed on blood, and a long slender proboscis to collect nectar from flowers.

COURTSHIP, BIRTH, AND GROWTH

REPRODUCTION is hazardous for insects. A female must first mate with a male of her own species and lay eggs where the newly hatched young can feed. The larvae must shed their skin several times as they grow. All this time the insects must avoid being eaten.

The light is produced by a chemical reaction.

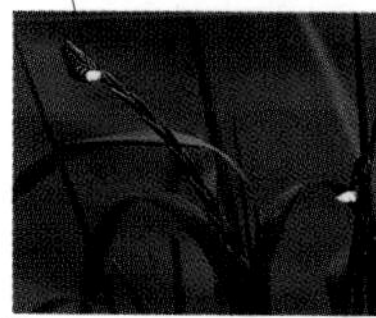

GUIDING LIGHT
Glowworms are the wingless females of certain beetle species. They attract males by producing a light near the tip of their abdomen. Some species flash a distinctive code to attract the correct males.

Courtship and mating

Males and females use special signals to ensure that their chosen mate is the right species. Courtship usually involves using scents, but may include color displays, dancing, caressing, and even gifts.

Butterflies find the scented chemicals, called pheromones, very attractive.

COURTSHIP FLIGHTS
Butterflies may recognize their own species by sight, but scent is more reliable. Butterfly courtship involves dancing flights with an exchange of scented chemical signals specific to each species.

MATING DANGER
Mating between some insect species may last for several hours, with the male gripping the female's abdomen with claspers. This keeps other males away, but the pair are vulnerable to predators at this time.

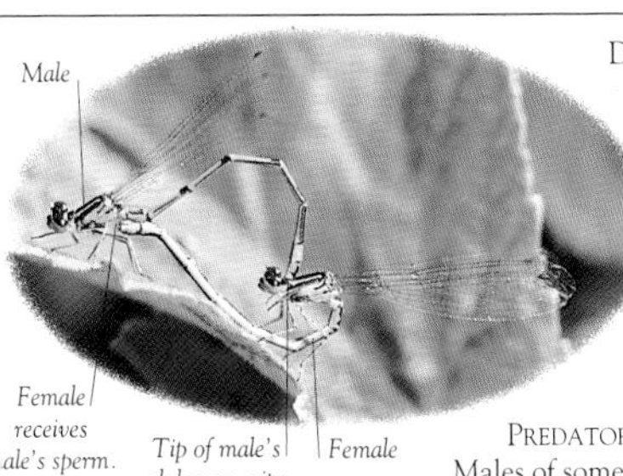

DAMSELFLIES

When mating, a male damselfly grips a female's neck with the tip of his abdomen. She receives a packet of sperm from a pouch near his legs; he continues to hold her neck while she lays eggs. This prevents other males from mating with her.

PREDATORS MATING

Males of some predatory species, such as empid flies, give the female a meal of a dead insect when mating so they are not eaten themselves. Some males trick the female. They give an empty parcel, and mate while the female opens it.

MATING ASIAN SWALLOWTAIL BUTTERFLIES

UNNATURAL BEHAVIOR

It is often said that a female mantis eats the male while he is mating with her. But this probably happens only when the mantises are in captivity and their behavior is not natural.

Eggs and egg-laying

Insects use up a lot of energy producing eggs. To make sure this energy is not wasted, insects have many ways of protecting their eggs from predators. A few species of insect stay with their eggs to protect them until the larvae hatch. Some insects lay their eggs underground with a supply of food waiting for the newly hatched larvae. Most insects lay their eggs either in or near food, so the young larvae do not have to travel far to eat.

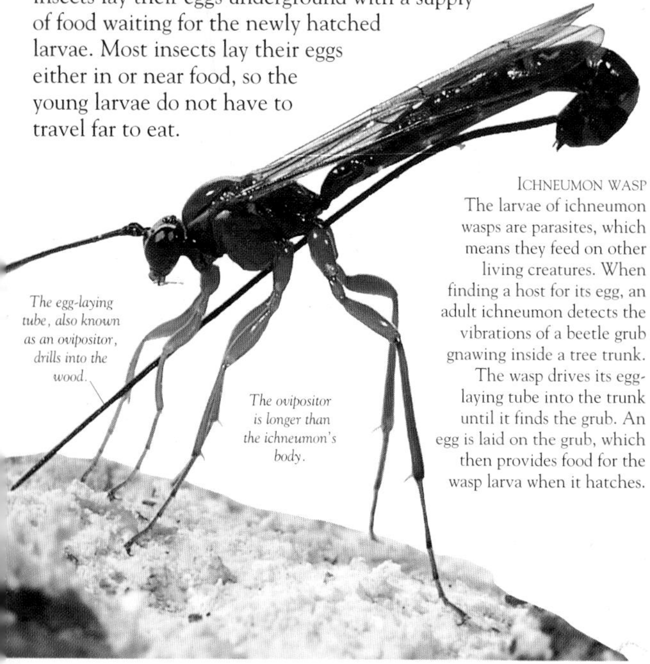

ICHNEUMON WASP
The larvae of ichneumon wasps are parasites, which means they feed on other living creatures. When finding a host for its egg, an adult ichneumon detects the vibrations of a beetle grub gnawing inside a tree trunk. The wasp drives its egg-laying tube into the trunk until it finds the grub. An egg is laid on the grub, which then provides food for the wasp larva when it hatches.

The egg-laying tube, also known as an ovipositor, drills into the wood.

The ovipositor is longer than the ichneumon's body.

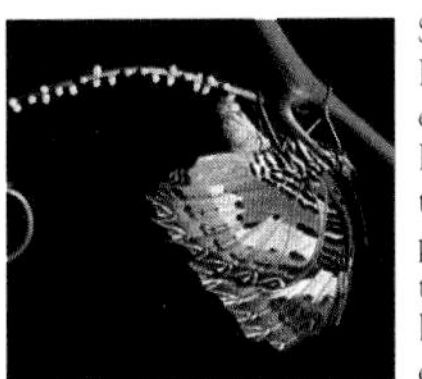

SUITABLE FOOD

Butterflies desert their eggs once they are laid. Different butterflies lay their eggs on different plants, depending on what the larvae eat. The Malay lacewing butterfly lays its eggs on vine tendrils.

Wasp carrying beetle to nest

Beetles are stored in underground nest.

CARING EARWIGS

A female earwig looks after her eggs, licking them regularly to keep them clean. When the nymphs hatch, she feeds them until they are big enough to leave the nest.

Earwig eggs

HUNTING WASPS

Most species of hunting wasp collect soft-bodied prey, such as caterpillars or spiders, for their grubs. But the weevil-hunting wasp collects adult beetles, which it stings and then stores in a tunnel as food for its larvae.

Vertical main tunnel

Beetles mold dung into balls.

Beetle fills tunnel with dung as food for newly hatched grubs.

DUNG BEETLES

The males and females of some dung beetle species work together to dig an underground tunnel with smaller tunnels branching off it. A female lays an egg in each of the smaller tunnels and fills them with animal dung, which the beetle grubs will feed on.

INSECT EGG FACTS

- Whitefly eggs have stalks that extract water from leaves.
- Tsetse flies develop their eggs internally and lay mature larvae.
- Green lacewing eggs have long stalks, making them difficult for predators to eat.

Birth and growth

As an insect grows from egg to adult it sheds its skin several times to produce a larger exoskeleton. While this new skin hardens the insect is soft and vulnerable. Insects have many life-cycle adaptations to protect their soft young stages.

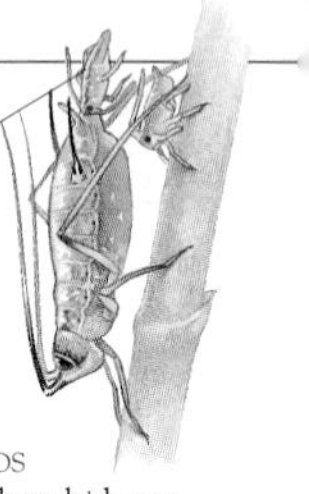

Newborn aphid

APHIDS

Female aphids can reproduce without mating. They give birth to live young rather than lay eggs, and each female may have about 100 offspring. The newborn aphids can give birth after only a few days.

EGGS

LARVA

PUPA

ADULT LADYBUG

LADYBUG GROWTH

Ladybugs and all other beetles go through a complete metamorphosis. An adult ladybug lays its eggs on a plant where small insects called aphids feed. Ladybug larvae eat aphids and shed their skin three times as they grow. The colorful adult emerges from the dull resting stage, or pupa.

FROTHY PROTECTION

Spittlebugs are soft-bodied bugs like aphids. A spittlebug nymph produces a frothy liquid from its anus. The froth protects the nymph from drying out, and also hides it from predators.

Frothy hideaway

PARENTAL CARE

The females of some species of shield bug stay with their eggs and young nymphs to protect them. If touched, the parent produces a powerful smell, giving these bugs the alternative name of stinkbugs.

SHIELD BUG NYMPHS WITH PARENT

BURROWING NYMPHS

A female locust can extend her abdomen to almost twice its length when laying eggs. The eggs are placed deep in the soil for protection. The newborn nymphs, called hoppers, must burrow to the surface to feed.

SPITTLEBUG NYMPH

LEAVING WATER

Unlike all other insects, mayflies have two adult stages. The first stage, the subadult, crawls out of the water where it lived as a nymph. It flies weakly and is dull colored. It soon molts to produce the true adult, which then mates.

Survival of the young

Predators eagerly hunt insect larvae since many are slow-moving, soft, and nutritious. To ensure survival, most insect species produc large numbers of young which grow rapidly. Most insect larvae are defenseless and have developed special ways of hiding from predators. But many insect larvae are fierce predators themselves, consuming other creatures for nourishment as they grow.

Grub in pupal cell

WELL HIDDEN
The larvae of chafer beetles live underground, safely hidden from most predators. The larvae, or grubs, may take many weeks to develop. They then produce a cell of hardened soil in which they will change into an adult.

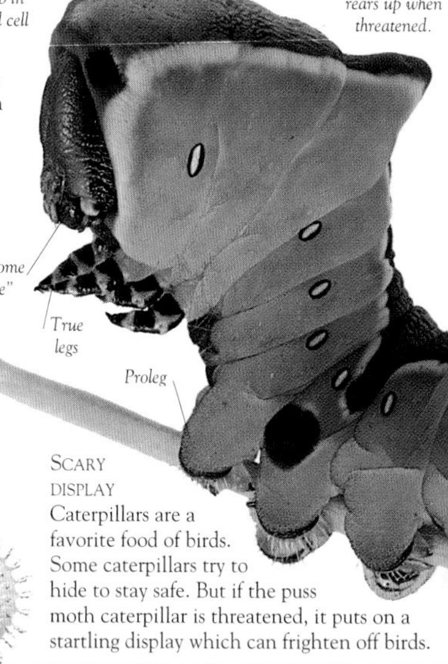

Sharp spines

SPINY LARVA
Mexican bean beetle larvae eat leaves and develop rapidly. They are covered with long, branched spines which may deter birds and other predators from attacking them.

SCARY DISPLAY
Caterpillars are a favorite food of birds. Some caterpillars try to hide to stay safe. But if the puss moth caterpillar is threatened, it puts on a startling display which can frighten off birds.

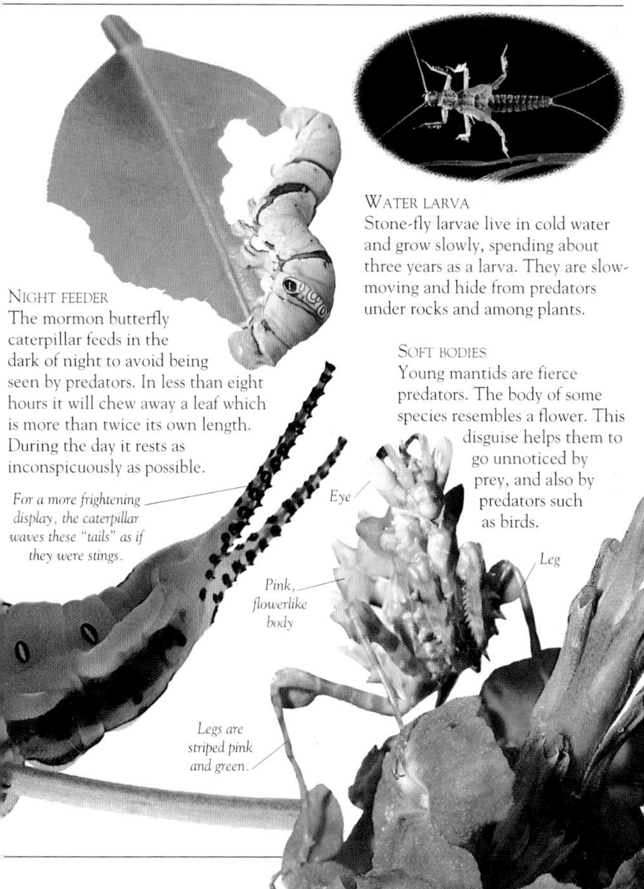

WATER LARVA
Stone-fly larvae live in cold water and grow slowly, spending about three years as a larva. They are slow-moving and hide from predators under rocks and among plants.

NIGHT FEEDER
The mormon butterfly caterpillar feeds in the dark of night to avoid being seen by predators. In less than eight hours it will chew away a leaf which is more than twice its own length. During the day it rests as inconspicuously as possible.

For a more frightening display, the caterpillar waves these "tails" as if they were stings.

SOFT BODIES
Young mantids are fierce predators. The body of some species resembles a flower. This disguise helps them to go unnoticed by prey, and also by predators such as birds.

Legs are striped pink and green.

NESTS AND SOCIETIES

MOST INSECTS lead solitary lives, but some, particularly wasps, ants, bees, and termites, live in societies which are sometimes very ordered. There are queens, kings, workers, and soldiers. Each of these has particular jobs to do. Social insects live in nests which are often elaborate, where they protect each other and rear their young.

TROPICAL WASP NEST MADE OF CHEWED-UP PLANT FIBERS

Wasps, ants, and bees

These insects produce a wide range of nests. Some are small with only a few dozen members, while larger nests may contain thousands of insects. Most have a single queen, and all the nest members are her offspring.

The nest is cemented together with wasp saliva.

ANTS

A species of African tree ant builds its nest from fragments of plants and soil to produce a substance like dark cement. The ants live on a diet of honeydew that they get from aphids. The aphids feed on the sap of leaves in the tree tops and discharge the honeydew from their rear ends.

BEES

A bumblebee queen starts her nest alone in spring in a hole in the ground. She makes cells for her eggs out of wax. She also makes a wax pot which she fills with honey for food.

The queen uses her antennae to measure the cells as she builds them.

1 A NEW START
European wasp colonies die out each winter. In spring a queen begins a new nest of "paper" made with chewed-up wood. She makes a few cells for her eggs, building walls around the cells to shield them.

Entrance hole

2 PROTECTIVE LAYERS
The queen builds more and more paper layers around the cells. The layers will protect the larvae from cold winds as well as from predators. The queen leaves an entrance hole at the bottom.

Finished nest

3 HARD-WORKING FAMILY
The first brood the queen rears become workers, gathering food for more larvae and expanding the nest. By summer, a nest may have 500 wasps, all collecting caterpillars for the larvae. A large nest may be as much as 18 in (45 cm) in diameter.

INSIDE THE NEST
The queen lays a single egg in each cell. When the larvae hatch they stay in their cell and the queen feeds them with pieces of caterpillar.

Termite nests

Termites have the most complex insect societies. Their elaborate nests, which may be in wood or underground, last for several years. Each nest has a single large queen and king, which are served by specialized small workers and large soldiers. Termites feed and protect each other, and one generation will help raise the next generation of offspring.

QUEEN TERMITE
In a termite society, the queen lays all the eggs. She is too fat to move, so the workers bring food to her. The queen lays 30,000 eggs each day and, as she lays them, the workers carry them off to special chambers for rearing.

Layers of "umbrellas"

NEST DEFENDERS
Termite soldiers fight enemies that attack the nest. Most termite species have soldiers with enlarged heads and powerful jaws. In some species, each soldier's head has a snout that squirts poison at invaders.

STRANGE NEST
The function of the "umbrellas" on this African nest is a mystery to scientists. The termite species that build this type of nest live underground. If an "umbrella" is damaged, it does not get repaired, but a new one may be built.

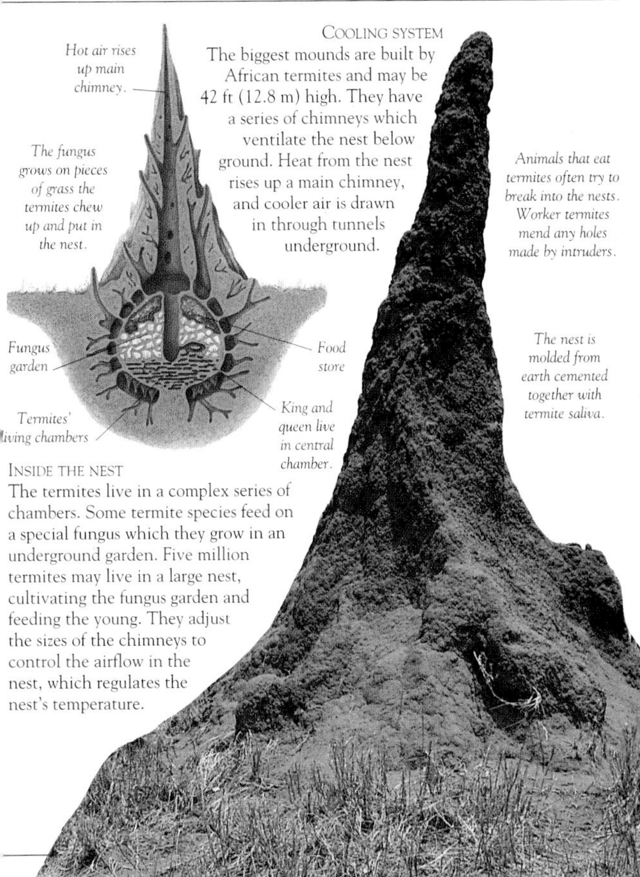

Hot air rises up main chimney.
The fungus grows on pieces of grass the termites chew up and put in the nest.
Fungus garden
Termites' living chambers
Food store
King and queen live in central chamber.
Animals that eat termites often try to break into the nests. Worker termites mend any holes made by intruders.
The nest is molded from earth cemented together with termite saliva.

COOLING SYSTEM

The biggest mounds are built by African termites and may be 42 ft (12.8 m) high. They have a series of chimneys which ventilate the nest below ground. Heat from the nest rises up a main chimney, and cooler air is drawn in through tunnels underground.

INSIDE THE NEST

The termites live in a complex series of chambers. Some termite species feed on a special fungus which they grow in an underground garden. Five million termites may live in a large nest, cultivating the fungus garden and feeding the young. They adjust the sizes of the chimneys to control the airflow in the nest, which regulates the nest's temperature.

HUNTING AND HIDING

SOME INSECT SPECIES are deadly hunters, killing prey with poisonous stings and sharp jaws. Insects are also hunted by a huge number of animals. To hide from predators, many insects have developed special disguises and patterns of behavior.

Hunting insects

About one-third of insect species are carnivorous (they eat meat). Some species eat decaying meat and dung, but most carnivorous insects hunt for their food.

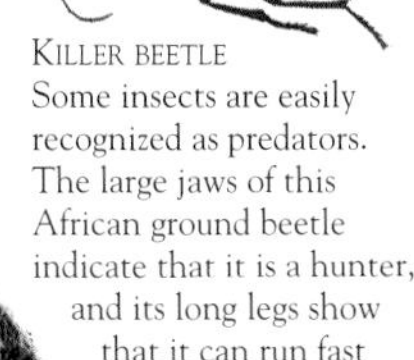

KILLER BEETLE
Some insects are easily recognized as predators. The large jaws of this African ground beetle indicate that it is a hunter, and its long legs show that it can run fast after its insect prey.

KILLER WASPS
There are many types of hunting wasp. Most adult hunting wasps are vegetarians – they hunt prey only as food for their larvae. Each hunting wasp species hunts a particular type of prey. The weevil-hunting wasp hunts only a type of beetle called a weevil.

Wasp cocoons

Wasp uses its antennae and sight to find cockroaches.

Beetle raises tail before attacking prey.

ESSENTIAL INSECTS

Ants are the most important carnivores on Earth. They eat huge numbers of other insects, which helps keep the insect population from becoming too plentiful. Ants in turn are eaten by other animals, such as birds and lizards.

PARASITES

The larvae of many species of wasp are parasites, which means they feed and grow inside another insect's body. This caterpillar has had about 50 wasp larvae feeding inside it. The larvae are pupating on the caterpillar's back. Soon they will hatch as adult wasps.

SPECIALIST HUNTER

Many predatory insects specialize on one particular type of prey. This jewel wasp hunts only cockroaches, which it uses as food for its larvae. The adult wasp is not carnivorous – it feeds on the nectar in flowers.

ROVE BEETLE

Some rove beetles specialize in feeding on springtails. To catch such elusive prey the beetle can flick out a long, sticky "tongue" to pull an unwary springtail into its mouth.

Camouflage

Insects whose body coloring matches their background are almost impossible to see. This method of hiding is known as camouflage. One of the first rules of successful camouflage is to keep still, since movement can betray an insect to a sharp-eyed predator. Some insects use another type of camouflage called disruptive coloration. They disguise their body by breaking up its shape with stripes and blocks of color.

GRASSY DISGUISE
The stripe-winged grasshopper can be heard singing in meadow grasses, but its camouflaged body is very hard to spot.

Grasshopper kicks any attackers with its back legs.

DISRUPTIVE COLORATION
This tropical moth has disruptive coloration. The patterns on the wings break up their shape. A predator might notice the patterns, but not the whole moth.

LOOKING DISTASTEFUL
This treehopper has twiglike extensions on its thorax and abdomen. It looks like an inedible piece of wood, so hunters are likely to overlook it.

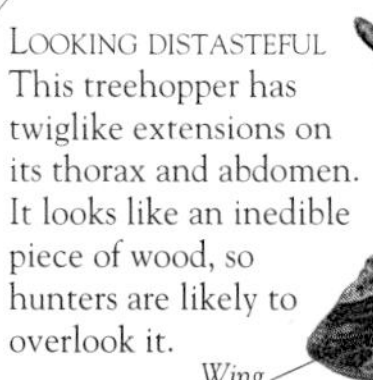

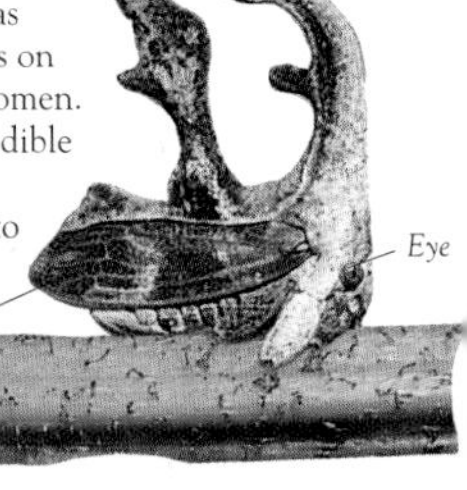

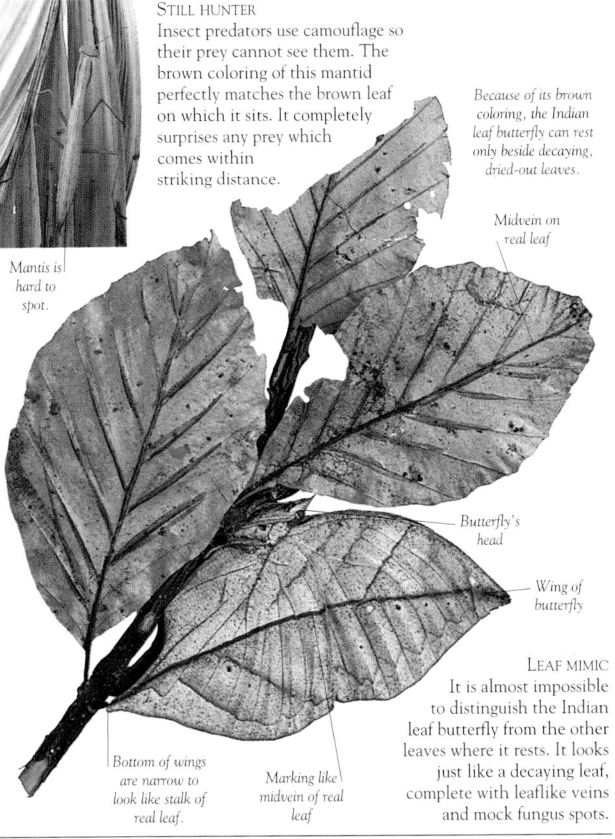
Mantis is hard to spot.
Because of its brown coloring, the Indian leaf butterfly can rest only beside decaying, dried-out leaves.
Midvein on real leaf
Butterfly's head
Wing of butterfly
Bottom of wings are narrow to look like stalk of real leaf.
Marking like midvein of real leaf

STILL HUNTER
Insect predators use camouflage so their prey cannot see them. The brown coloring of this mantid perfectly matches the brown leaf on which it sits. It completely surprises any prey which comes within striking distance.

LEAF MIMIC
It is almost impossible to distinguish the Indian leaf butterfly from the other leaves where it rests. It looks just like a decaying leaf, complete with leaflike veins and mock fungus spots.

Warning coloration

Birds, mammals, and other intelligent predators learn through experience that some insects are poisonous or harmful. Such insects do not camouflage themselves. Instead they have brightly colored bodies which warn predators that they have an unpleasant taste or a nasty sting. The most common warning colors are red, yellow, and black. Any insect with those colors is probably poisonous.

BASKER MOTH
Moths that fly by day are often brightly colored, particularly when they taste unpleasant. The red, yellow, and black coloring of this basker moth tells birds that it is not a tasty meal.

PAINFUL REMINDER
The saddle-back caterpillar is eye-catching with its vivid coloring and grotesque appearance. No young bird would ever forget the caterpillar if it tried a mouthful of the poisonous, stinging spines.

Poisonous spines

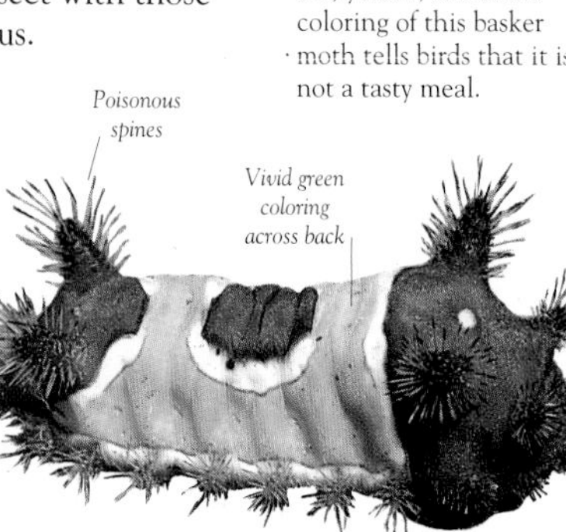

Vivid green coloring across back

Bright spot

WARNING SPOTS
This assassin bug is easily seen because of the two bright spots on its back. These bold markings warn predators that there is a reason for them to stay away. The bug's weapon is a needle-sharp beak which can give a very painful bite.

EYESPOTS

This silkmoth is camouflaged when its wings are closed. But when attacked by a predator, the moth flashes the eyespots on its hind wings. This startles the attacker briefly, and may give the moth time to escape.

POISONOUS BODY

This grasshopper tastes horrible. It gets its terrible flavor from eating poisonous plants and storing the poisons in its body. The yellow and black stripes advertise its unpleasantness to birds and other predators.

Camouflaged front wings
Eyespot
Eyes are black to blend with rest of coloring.
Grasshopper uses the spines on its legs to grip plants.

Mimicry

Predators usually avoid preying on dangerous animals. Many harmless insects take advantage of this by mimicking harmful creatures. Mimicking insects copy a dangerous animal's body shape and coloring. They also behave like the animal they're copying to make the disguise more convincing. Inedible objects, such as twigs and thorns, are also mimicked by insects.

The treehoppers move only when they need a fresh source of food.

Markings make head resemble alligator's head.

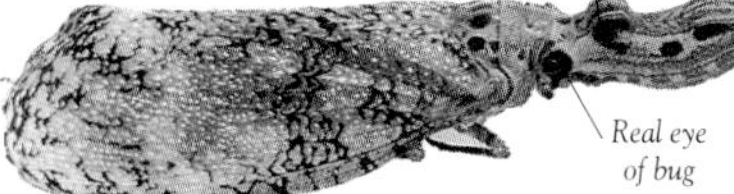

Real eye of bug

ALLIGATOR MIMIC

Scientists can often only guess at the reasons for the strange look and behavior of some animals. It is not known why this tree-living bug looks like a tiny alligator. Perhaps its appearance briefly startles monkey predators, giving the bug time to fly off to safety.

HORNET MIMIC

The hornet moth looks very like the large wasp called a hornet. When flying, it even behaves like a hornet. Many insects find protection by mimicking wasps – birds avoid them because they might sting.

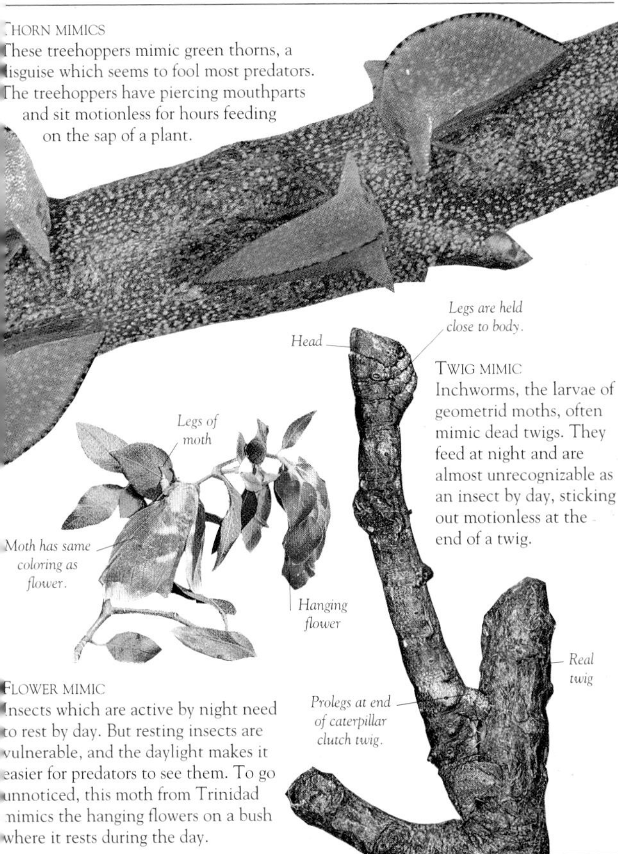
Legs are held close to body.
Head
Legs of moth
Moth has same coloring as flower.
Hanging flower
Real twig
Prolegs at end of caterpillar clutch twig.

THORN MIMICS

These treehoppers mimic green thorns, a disguise which seems to fool most predators. The treehoppers have piercing mouthparts and sit motionless for hours feeding on the sap of a plant.

TWIG MIMIC

Inchworms, the larvae of geometrid moths, often mimic dead twigs. They feed at night and are almost unrecognizable as an insect by day, sticking out motionless at the end of a twig.

FLOWER MIMIC

Insects which are active by night need to rest by day. But resting insects are vulnerable, and the daylight makes it easier for predators to see them. To go unnoticed, this moth from Trinidad mimics the hanging flowers on a bush where it rests during the day.

WHERE INSECTS LIVE

INSECTS LIVE everywhere there is warmth and moisture. Many of the one million or more species have specialized habitat requirements. They can live only in particular places, and easily become extinct when humans change or destroy their surroundings. Other species are able to adapt to changing conditions; these adaptable insects often become pests.

NORTH AMERICA

SOUTH AMERICA

TEMPERATE WOODLAND
The varied plant life and complex structure of temperate woodland provides insects with many different habitats. Trees, shrubs, and herbs all have flowers, fruits, and buds for insects to feed on, as well as stems and roots for insects to bore into.

GRASSLANDS AND HEATHLANDS
These habitats offer little shelter from bad weather. But they warm up quickly in the sun, and have a rich variety of flowering plants.

TOWNS AND GARDENS
Hundreds of insect species take advantage of human habitats. Insects find food and shelter in our roofs, cellars, food stores, kitchens, garbage cans, farms, and in our flower-filled gardens.

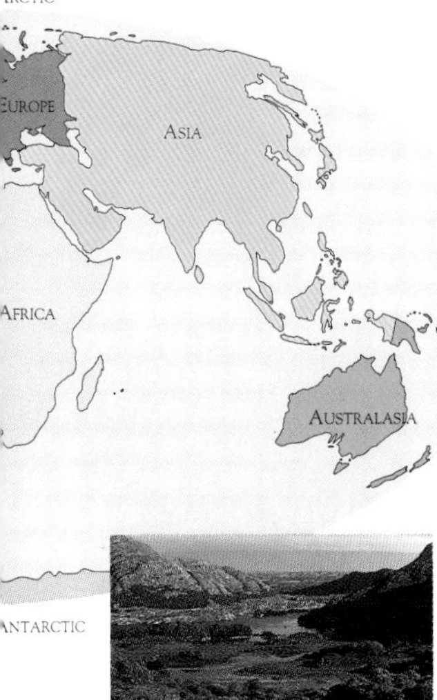

LAKES AND RIVERS
Freshwater insects are highly specialized. Their bodies have modified to allow them to swim and breathe underwater.

DESERTS, CAVES, AND SOIL
These are inhospitable habitats. Food and water are scarce in deserts. Caves are dark and cold. It is hard for insects to move and communicate in dense soil.

TROPICAL FORESTS
This is the richest habitat for insect species. Thousands of species of plants provide countless niches for insects to live in, from treetop fruits to dead leaves and twigs on the ground.

TEMPERATE WOODLAND

TEMPERATE WOODLANDS are often dominated by one tree species, such as oak, which is deciduous (the trees lose their leaves in winter). The types of insect found, and their numbers, will vary with the seasons, as well as with the types of tree species in the woodlands.

FIELD SCABIOUS FLOWER

DRAINING
Forests in wetlands have many different plant species. But people often drain this habitat because it is good for farming. Draining kills plants such as milk-parsley, the only plant the English swallowtail butterfly will breed on. This beautiful insect is now rarely seen.

Although the English swallowtail will lay eggs only on milk-parsley, adults eat a variety of flowers.

WOODLAND FACTS

- The woodland edge supports the greatest number of insect species.
- Each pair of blue tits needs about 5,000 caterpillars to feed to their chicks.
- In Britain, over 280 species of insect live on native oak trees.
- Temperate rainforests in the northwestern United States are disappearing faster than tropical rainforests.

Bumblebees are very common in woodlands.

+2

FLOWERS

Woodlands contain many types of flower. These attract various species of insect, such as bumblebees, which nest in the ground in animal burrows and pollinate many woodland flowers.

Vaporer moth caterpillar is covered with tufts of hair.

VAPORER MOTH CATERPILLAR

This attractive caterpillar eats the leaves of many different trees in Europe and North America. It will also attack rosebushes and heather plants.

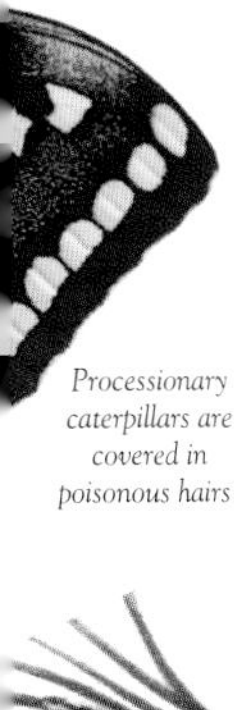

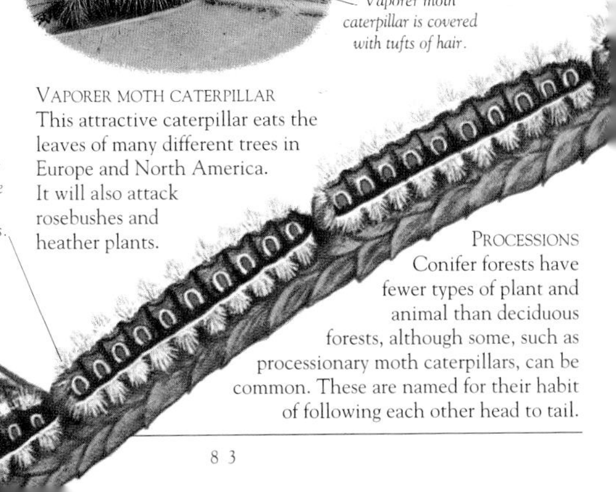

Processionary caterpillars are covered in poisonous hairs.

PROCESSIONS

Conifer forests have fewer types of plant and animal than deciduous forests, although some, such as processionary moth caterpillars, can be common. These are named for their habit of following each other head to tail.

OAK TREE

IN NORTH AMERICA and Europe, oak trees support a rich variety of insects. There are insects living on every part of the oak tree – the leaves, buds, flowers, fruits, wood, bark, and on decaying leaves and branches. All these insects provide food for the many birds and other animals found in oak woodland.

OAK TREE

GREEN OAK TORTRIX MOTH

+1.25

CATERPILLAR

+2

GREEN OAK TORTRIX

The green wings of the green oak tortrix moth camouflage the moth when it rests on a leaf. Green oak tortrix caterpillars are extremely common on oak trees. The caterpillars hide from hungry predators by rolling themselves up in a leaf.

Leaf rolled around green oak tortrix caterpillar

Mine

MAKING A TUNNEL

The caterpillars of some small moths tunnel between the upper and lower surfaces of a leaf. They eat the green tissues between these surfaces as they tunnel, and leave a see-through trail called a mine.

GALLS

Oak trees have many tiny growths called galls. Galls are grown by the tree around eggs laid by gall wasps. When the eggs hatch, the gall provides food and shelter for up to 30 wasp larvae. Parasitic wasps called chalcid wasps sometimes burrow inside galls and lay their eggs beside the gall wasp eggs. When the chalcid larvae hatch they eat the gall wasp larvae.

NUT WEEVILS

Acorns are used as food by nut weevils. They drill a hole in an acorn with their long, thin snout, and then lay their eggs inside. The larvae feed inside the acorn, and this turns the acorn black.

TREE CANOPY

THE UPPER BRANCHES and leaves of a tree are like a living green umbrella, forming a canopy over the lower plants. Countless insects find their food in the canopy and they are food for many different birds.

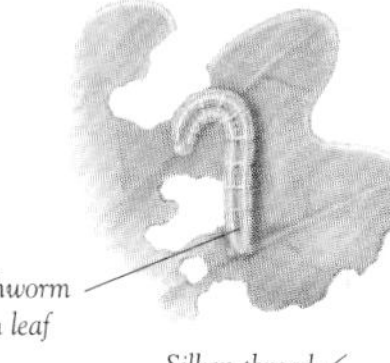

Inchworm on leaf

Silken thread suspends inchworm.

INCHWORMS
Some young birds like to feed on inchworms, the caterpillars of Geometrid moths. When in danger, inchworms can drop from a leaf and hang below by a silken thread.

Very long antennae help the cricket find its way in the dark. They also alert the cricket to the approach of an enemy.

Compound eye

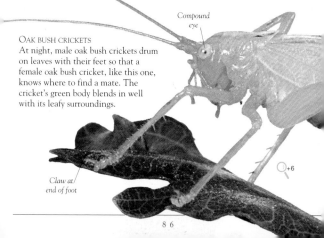

OAK BUSH CRICKETS
At night, male oak bush crickets drum on leaves with their feet so that a female oak bush cricket, like this one, knows where to find a mate. The cricket's green body blends in well with its leafy surroundings.

+6

Claw at end of foot

Wasps kill insects that destroy plants and fruit.

WASPS
A healthy woodland has a balance of prey and predators. Wasps grow up on a diet of chewed caterpillars collected in the tree canopy. In summer a wasp nest may contain several hundred wasps.

Claw on end of foot for gripping surfaces

EUROPEAN WASP

MALE PURPLE EMPEROR AT REST

PURPLE EMPEROR
The territory of a male purple emperor is often at the top of the tallest tree in a wood. If a rival male enters another male's territory, the two fight in midair, batting wings until one gives in.

Camouflaged underside of wings

Strong back legs can be used to kick enemies.

MALE PURPLE EMPEROR

Wings are normally dark brown.

It is only when wings are at a certain angle to the light that they appear to be purple.

WOODLAND BUTTERFLIES

THE RICH VARIETY of habitats in woodlands supports many butterfly species. Some live in the canopy; others feed on low shrubs. But most butterflies need sunshine and can be found on flowers in sunny clearings.

–.5

SILVER-WASHED FRITILLARY
This butterfly lays its eggs in cracks in the bark of mossy tree trunks, close to where violets are growing. The caterpillars feed on the leaves of these plants.

Brown upperside

–.7

Green underside

GREEN HAIRSTREAK
Whether it is sitting on a branch or resting on a leaf, the green hairstreak butterfly is well camouflaged. Its upperside is a woody brown while its underside is a leafy green.

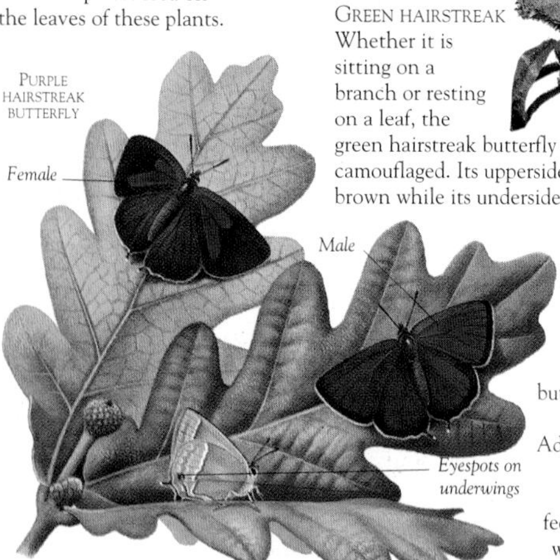

PURPLE HAIRSTREAK
High in the canopy of oak trees the caterpillars of the purple hairstreak butterfly feed on flowers and young leaves. Adult purple hairstreaks spend most of their lives in the treetops, feeding and sunbathing with their wings open.

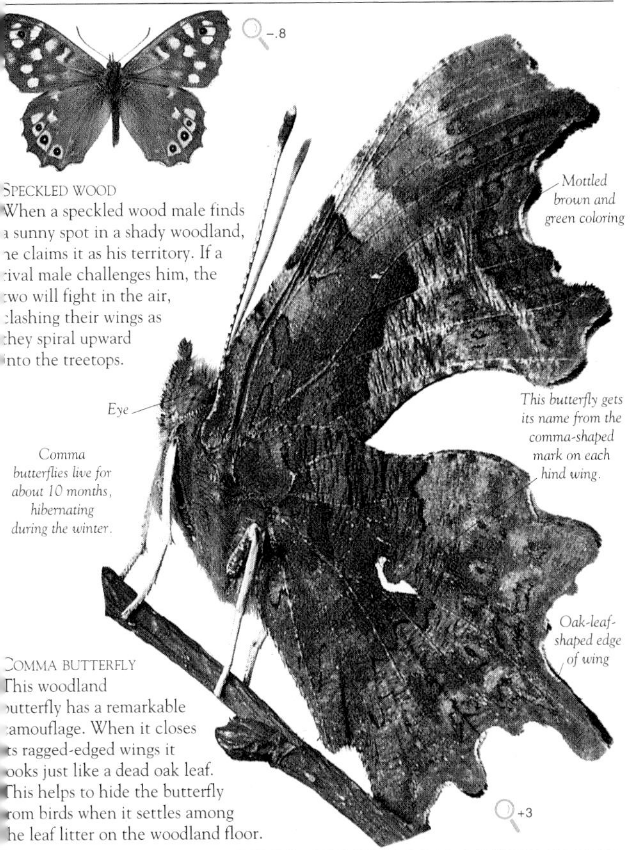

SPECKLED WOOD
When a speckled wood male finds a sunny spot in a shady woodland, he claims it as his territory. If a rival male challenges him, the two will fight in the air, clashing their wings as they spiral upward into the treetops.

Comma butterflies live for about 10 months, hibernating during the winter.

COMMA BUTTERFLY
This woodland butterfly has a remarkable camouflage. When it closes its ragged-edged wings it looks just like a dead oak leaf. This helps to hide the butterfly from birds when it settles among the leaf litter on the woodland floor.

TREE TRUNKS AND BRANCHES

CRACKS IN THE bark of trees provide a hiding place for many species of insect. Some burrow into the wood and live completely concealed from predators. Many insects also live and feed among the different plant life that grows on tree trunks and branches.

BARK INSECTS
Insects which live on bark are usually camouflaged, such as barklice, which feed on tiny fungi and algae. Another bark insect, the snakefly, is a predator. When it hunts, it looks like a tiny snake about to strike, holding its head high looking for prey.

+4

BARKLOUSE
Mesopsocus

+1.5

SNAKEFLY

+2.7

BARKLOUSE
Loensia fasciata

WOOD WASP
This female giant wood wasp has a long, stout egg-laying tube, or ovipositor, which looks like a fearsome sting. It lays eggs deep inside the soft wood of dead or dying trees.

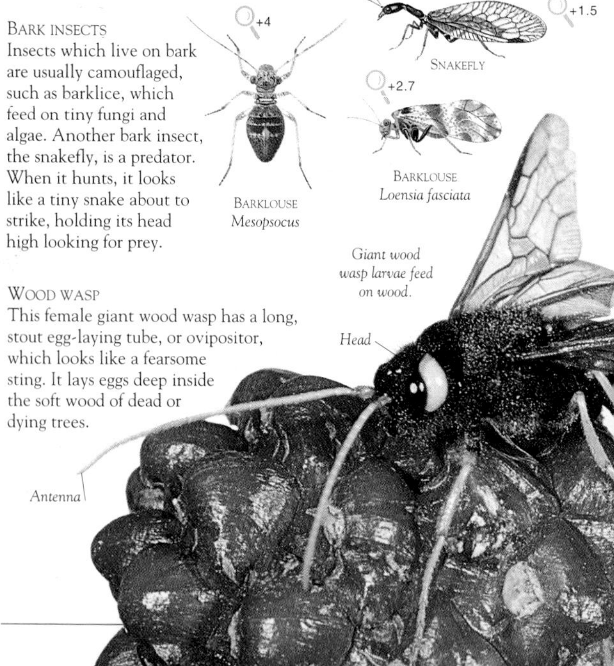
Giant wood wasp larvae feed on wood.
Head
Antenna

Elm bark beetle

A female elm bark beetle lays eggs along a tunnel which she bores in the bark of an elm tree. The larvae feed on the inner surface of the bark, creating radiating tunnels as they feed and grow.

Moth camouflaged on lichen

Tunnels which larvae have created

Eggs are laid in central tunnel.

The merveille du jour moth is easy to see when not on lichen.

Ovipositor bores into wood where it deposits eggs.

Merveille moth

The patterns on the front wings of the merveille du jour moth help to camouflage it when it rests on lichens growing on a tree trunk. The moth is active at night and rests during the day. Its camouflage has to be good to hide it in bright daylight from predators such as birds and lizards.

GROUND LEVEL

THE WOODLAND floor does not get much sunlight, so few plants grow there. Most insects at ground level feed on plant and animal debris falling from the canopy, or, if they are carnivorous, eat other insects.

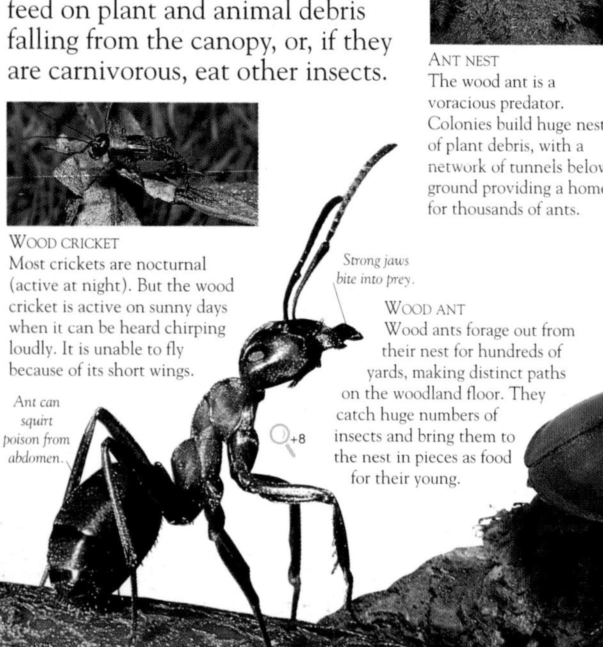
Strong jaws bite into prey.
Ant can squirt poison from abdomen.
+8

ANT NEST
The wood ant is a voracious predator. Colonies build huge nests of plant debris, with a network of tunnels below ground providing a home for thousands of ants.

WOOD CRICKET
Most crickets are nocturnal (active at night). But the wood cricket is active on sunny days when it can be heard chirping loudly. It is unable to fly because of its short wings.

WOOD ANT
Wood ants forage out from their nest for hundreds of yards, making distinct paths on the woodland floor. They catch huge numbers of insects and bring them to the nest in pieces as food for their young.

−1
+2.5
Antenna
Only male stag beetles have enlarged jaws.
+3

UPPERSIDE OF WHITE ADMIRAL

UNDERSIDE OF WHITE ADMIRAL

'IOLET GROUND BEETLE

'his beetle can run fast n its long legs, catching ther insects among the eaf litter. It hunts mainly t night and grips its prey 'ith powerful jaws.

WHITE ADMIRALS

On sunny days, white admiral butterflies can be spotted near the ground feeding on the nectar of bramble flowers. They can often be seen in the morning sipping water from puddles. They spend much of their time in the tree canopy, basking in the sunshine.

'TAG BEETLE

'he larvae of stag beetles spend about hree years feeding on rotting wood nside a dead tree. These handsome eetles are now becoming rare ecause dead wood is often leared away and burned.

GRASSLANDS AND HEATHLANDS

HERE, THE LACK OF PROTECTIVE tree canopy results in quick changes in the weather. Grassland and heathland habitats provide fewer dwelling places for insects than forest or woodland, since there is little wood to burrow into and hardly any leaf litter to dwell in.

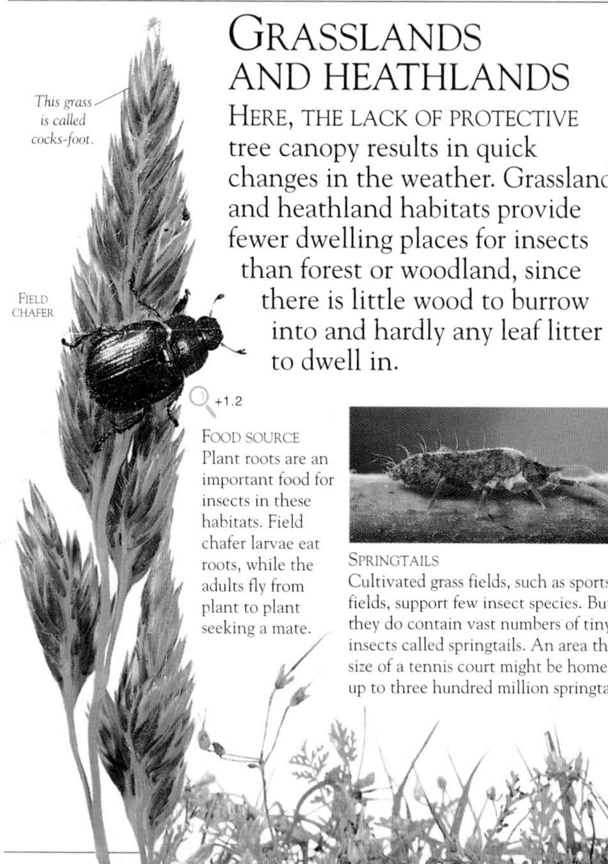

This grass is called cocks-foot.

FIELD CHAFER

FOOD SOURCE
Plant roots are an important food for insects in these habitats. Field chafer larvae eat roots, while the adults fly from plant to plant seeking a mate.

SPRINGTAILS
Cultivated grass fields, such as sports fields, support few insect species. But they do contain vast numbers of tiny insects called springtails. An area the size of a tennis court might be home to up to three hundred million springtails.

OXFORD RAGWORT
A weed called the Oxford ragwort is a common invader of neglected pasture in Europe. The cinnabar moth lays its eggs on this weed, and its caterpillars eat the leaves.

CINNABAR MOTH

–.8

The moth has warning coloration because it tastes unpleasant.

An Oxford ragwort is often stripped of its leaves by feeding caterpillars.

GRASSLAND AND HEATHLAND FACTS

- The grasslands of Argentina are called Pampas, or "plains" in the language of the native people.
- Prairies of the US have tall grasses.
- Steppes (prairielike land) of Siberia have short grasses.

RICH IN PLANT LIFE
Natural grassland and heathland have a huge variety of grasses and flowering plants. These rich habitats buzz with insect life in the summer months.

CRANESBILL

EXTINCT BUTTERFLY
The English large copper butterfly was once common in fenland but is now extinct. This is a result of intensive land development for agriculture, which destroyed the butterfly's special food plant.

GRASSLAND INSECTS

MOST INSECT species cannot survive in cultivated grasslands, such as garden lawns, since they usually contain only one type of grass. Also, weedkillers and other chemicals harm many insects. But natural grasslands, with their variety of plants, support thousands of insect species that have adapted to this open, windy habitat.

DUNG BEETLES
These beetles are common in grasslands where cattle graze. Dung beetles lay their eggs in animal dung which their larvae feed on when they hatch. The adults collect the dung by molding it into balls, then roll it to their underground burrows.

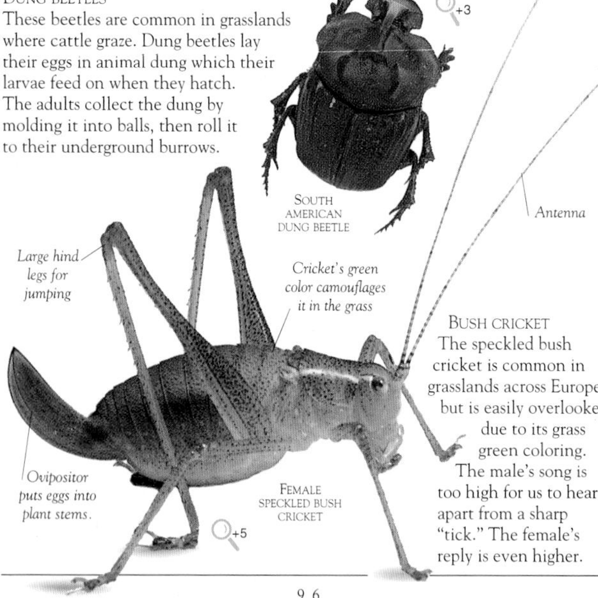
+3
Antenna
Large hind legs for jumping
Cricket's green color camouflages it in the grass
Ovipositor puts eggs into plant stems.
+5

SOUTH AMERICAN DUNG BEETLE

FEMALE SPECKLED BUSH CRICKET

BUSH CRICKET
The speckled bush cricket is common in grasslands across Europe, but is easily overlooked due to its grass green coloring. The male's song is too high for us to hear, apart from a sharp "tick." The female's reply is even higher.

NTEATER
here are so many ants in
ie grasslands of South
merica and Africa
iat specialized
nt-eating
ammals have
volved. They have
owerful claws to break open ant
ests, and long sticky tongues to
ollect the ants.

ANTEATER

LARGE BLUE BUTTERFLY
This butterfly lays its eggs on the wild thyme plant, and the newly hatched caterpillars feed on thyme flowers. The caterpillars attract red ants with a special milk. The ants are deceived into carrying the caterpillars into their nest, where the caterpillars eat the ant eggs and larva.

Ragwort flowers

Mating soldier beetles

ARBLED WHITE BUTTERFLY
his butterfly can be found in a
riety of grassland habitats, including
assy areas inside woodland. Marbled
hites often gather in groups to
sk in the early morning and
rly evening sunshine.

OLDIER BEETLES
ome insects feed on one particular
ower, while others, such as
ldier beetles, eat pollen from
arious flowers. These feeding
tes are also good places for
sects to find a mate.

HEATHLAND INSECTS

MANY BURROWING insects live in heathlan since the soil is loose and easy to dig into. Heathland occurs in parts of the world with a climate of rainy winters and warm, dry summers. It has a rich mixture of plants, and the soil, which is often sandy, warms up quickly in the sunshine.

Butterfly is hard to spot in the grass.

GRAYLING BUTTERFLY
The tops of the wings of the grayling butterfly are brightl colored, while their undersid is mottled gray for camouflag on the ground. When resting it folds back its wings and sometimes leans toward the sun so it casts no shadow.

COMMON YELLOW DUNG FLY

+4

Dung flies eat other insects, which they kill with piercing mouthparts.

DUNG FLY
Wherever cattle are grazing, insects will b found breeding in the cattle's nutritious dung. Dung flies lay their eggs on freshly deposited cow pats. The maggots hatch a few hours later and start eating the dung.

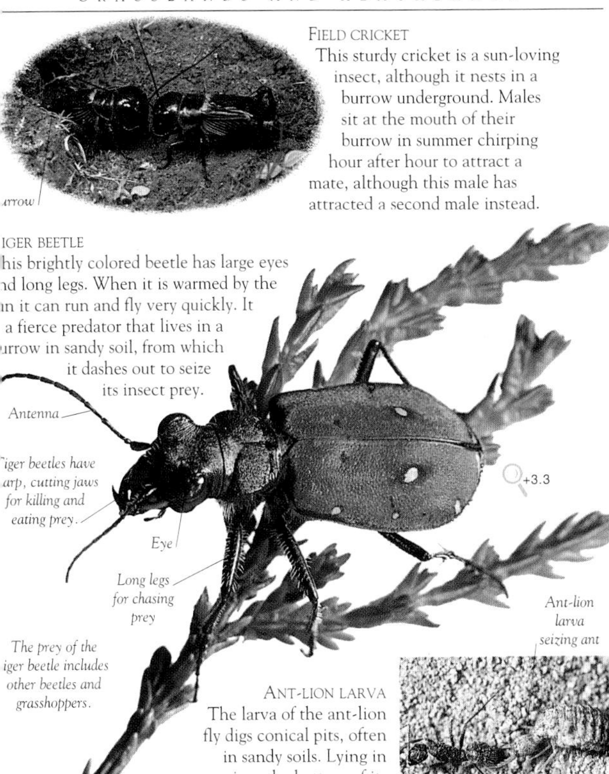
urrow
Antenna
'iger beetles have
arp, cutting jaws
for killing and
eating prey.
Eye
Long legs
for chasing
prey
+3.3
The prey of the
iger beetle includes
other beetles and
grasshoppers.
Ant-lion
larva
seizing ant

FIELD CRICKET

This sturdy cricket is a sun-loving insect, although it nests in a burrow underground. Males sit at the mouth of their burrow in summer chirping hour after hour to attract a mate, although this male has attracted a second male instead.

IGER BEETLE

his brightly colored beetle has large eyes ıd long legs. When it is warmed by the ın it can run and fly very quickly. It a fierce predator that lives in a ırrow in sandy soil, from which it dashes out to seize its insect prey.

ANT-LION LARVA

The larva of the ant-lion fly digs conical pits, often in sandy soils. Lying in wait at the bottom of its pit, the larva uses its long jaws to catch any small insect that falls in.

LAKES AND RIVERS

INSECTS CAN be found in all sorts of freshwater habitats: lakes, fast-flowing streams, ponds, puddles, damp moss, and wet leaf litter. These insects have many adaptations for surviving in their watery homes.

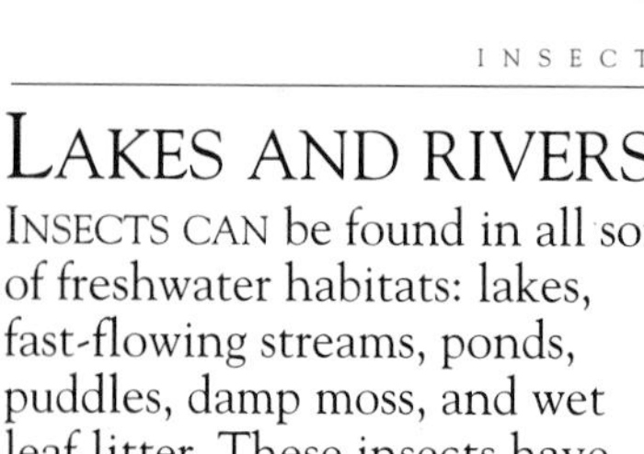

This case is made of a mixture of leaves and stones.

The stony case is held together by silk woven by the larva.

Head

Legs hold onto plant.

CADDIS FLY LARVAE
Insects are in danger of bein swept away in fast-flowin water. Caddis f larvae build a case around their body fo protection, and often the cases are mad of heavy stone to weigh the larvae dowr

Flowers attract nectar-eating insects.

The flat leaves have a water-repellent waxy covering so they don't get waterlogged.

FRINGED WATERLILY
The tangled stems of the fringed waterlily are a good hiding place for pond insects. Dragonflies also find the leaves and stems a safe place on which to lay their eggs.

GILLS

A caddis fly larva has gills for taking oxygen from the water. The larva undulates its body to create a flow of oxygen-rich water over its gills inside the case.

WATER SCORPION

The water scorpion has a breathing tube on its rear end so it can breathe the outside air while it is underwater. Insects with breathing tubes can survive in warm ponds or polluted waters that are low in oxygen.

SPRINGTAILS

In corners of ponds sheltered from the wind, swarms of springtails sometimes gather on the surface of the water. They feed on organic debris that has blown into the pond.

FAST STREAMS

Insects that live in fast-flowing streams have streamlined bodies and strong claws to help them cling to stones. The water that passes over their gills is always rich in oxygen, but cool temperatures mean that larvae develop more slowly than they would in a shallow, sun-warmed pond.

LAKES AND RIVERS FACTS

- Fish populations depend on plenty of insects as food.
- Dragonfly larvae are considered a delicacy in New Guinea.
- Swarms of nonbiting midges are sometimes so dense over African lakes that fishermen have been suffocated.

WATER SURFACE INSECTS

A WATER SURFACE behaves like a skin due to a force called surface tension. This force enables certain insects to walk on the "skin," and others to hang just beneath it. Many of these insects are predators, and much of their food comes from the constant supply of flying insects which have fallen into the water.

+6

WHIRLIGIG
The whirligig beetle swims around and around very fast on the water surface. It hunts insects trapped on the surface tension. The whirligig's eyes are divided into two halves, allowing it to see both above and below the water surface at the same time.

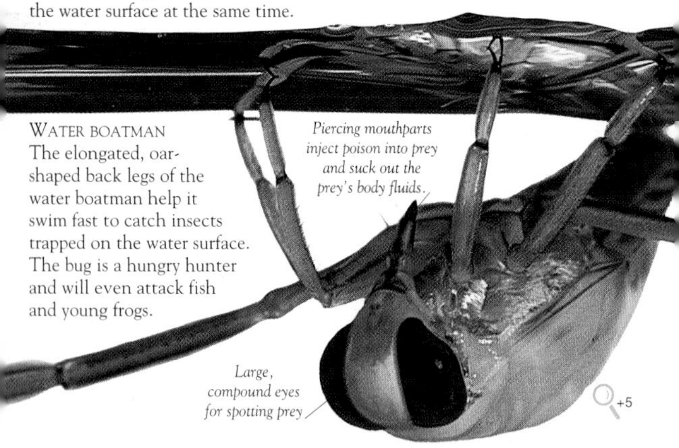

WATER BOATMAN
The elongated, oar-shaped back legs of the water boatman help it swim fast to catch insects trapped on the water surface. The bug is a hungry hunter and will even attack fish and young frogs.

Piercing mouthparts inject poison into prey and suck out the prey's body fluids.

Large, compound eyes for spotting prey

+5

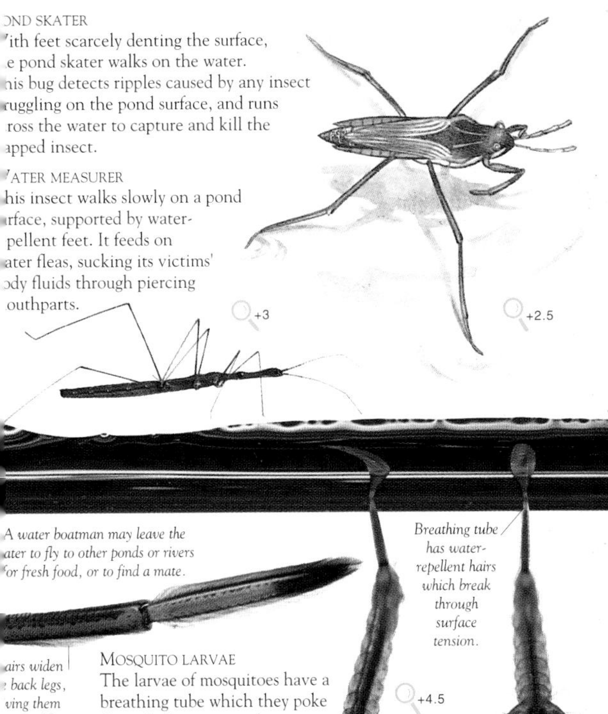

ƆND SKATER

'ith feet scarcely denting the surface, e pond skater walks on the water. his bug detects ripples caused by any insect ruggling on the pond surface, and runs ross the water to capture and kill the apped insect.

'ATER MEASURER

his insect walks slowly on a pond ırface, supported by water-pellent feet. It feeds on ater fleas, sucking its victims' ɔdy fluids through piercing outhparts.

A water boatman may leave the ater to fly to other ponds or rivers 'or fresh food, or to find a mate.

airs widen : back legs, ving them eir oarlike shape.

Breathing tube has water-repellent hairs which break through surface tension.

MOSQUITO LARVAE

The larvae of mosquitoes have a breathing tube which they poke through the water surface. The larvae are legless and swim by wriggling, rising to the surface now and again to take air.

Underwater insects

Many of the insects that live underwater are carnivorous, either hunting their prey or scavenging. Some of these insects are fierce, sometimes killing prey larger than themselves.

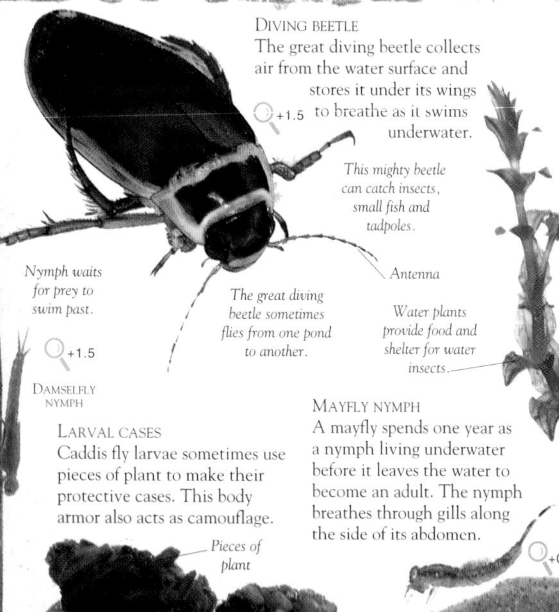

Diving beetle

The great diving beetle collects air from the water surface and stores it under its wings to breathe as it swims underwater.

This mighty beetle can catch insects, small fish and tadpoles.

Nymph waits for prey to swim past.

The great diving beetle sometimes flies from one pond to another.

Water plants provide food and shelter for water insects.

Damselfly nymph

Larval cases

Caddis fly larvae sometimes use pieces of plant to make their protective cases. This body armor also acts as camouflage.

Mayfly nymph

A mayfly spends one year as a nymph living underwater before it leaves the water to become an adult. The nymph breathes through gills along the side of its abdomen.

ADULT DRAGONFLY

Male darter dragonflies perch on plants that emerge from the water. They fiercely attack and drive away any rival males of the same species, but attempt to mate with any female darter dragonfly that flies past.

DRAGONFLY EGGS

Darter dragonflies scatter their eggs in the water. The eggs are surrounded by a sticky, jelly-like substance, and hatch after a few days.

Jelly holds eggs in place.

−.7

BEETLE LARVA

The larva of the great diving beetle njects juices into prey with its jaws. The juices turn the prey's insides nto liquid for the larva to suck out.

DRAGONFLY NYMPH

Dragonfly nymphs breathe by pumping water in and out of their rear end, where they have complex gills.

+1.5

ORCHID

TROPICAL FOREST

INSECTS THRIVE in the humid heat and flourishing plant life of tropica forests. These forests have a complex structure that provides many habitats for insects. Trees vary in shape and size; vines and dead branches are everywhere, and thick leaf litter covers the ground.

ORCHIDS
Tropical forests contain a spectacular variety of plants – there are about 25,000 species of orchid alone. It is quite dark beneath the forest canopy and orchids are strongly scented to help insects find them.

EPIPHYTES
Many plants grow on the trunks and branches of trees where birds have wiped seeds from their beaks. These tree-dwelling plants, called epiphytes, provide extra habitats for insects.

INSECT PREDATORS
A tropical forest is a rich habitat for birds as well as insects. Tropical birds feed on countless insects each day. This high rate of predation is a major reason for the evolution of camouflage and mimicry in tropical insects.

FRUITY NOURISHMENT
Some tropical butterflies live for several months. An important source of fuel for their continued activity is rotting fruit and dung on the forest floor. This gives them not only sugars for energy, but also amino acids and vitamins needed for survival.

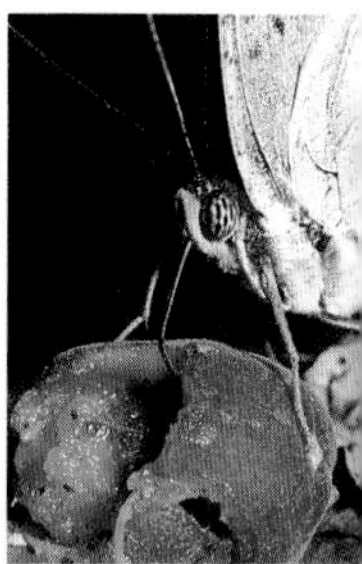

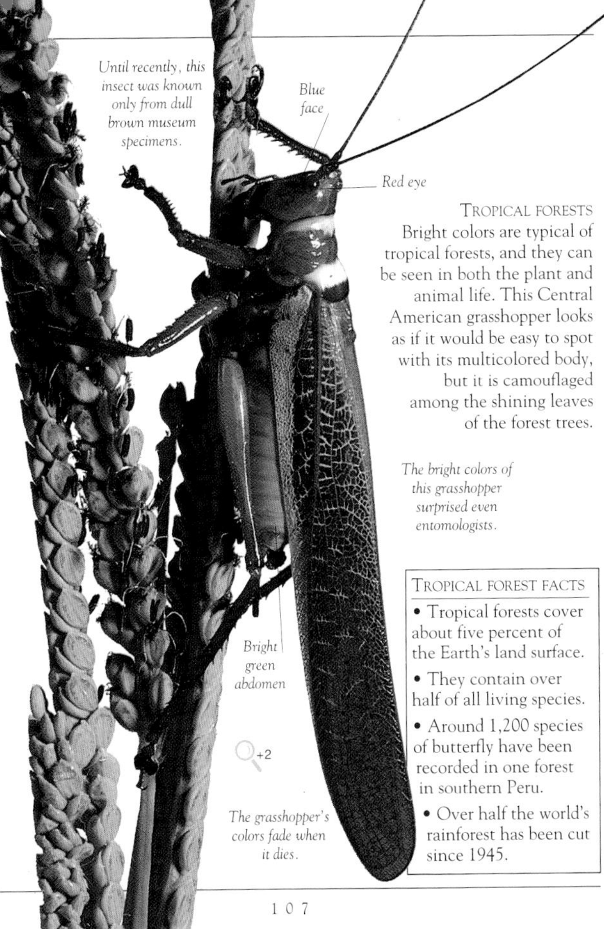

Until recently, this insect was known only from dull brown museum specimens.
Blue face
Red eye
The bright colors of this grasshopper surprised even entomologists.
Bright green abdomen
+2
The grasshopper's colors fade when it dies.

TROPICAL FORESTS

Bright colors are typical of tropical forests, and they can be seen in both the plant and animal life. This Central American grasshopper looks as if it would be easy to spot with its multicolored body, but it is camouflaged among the shining leaves of the forest trees.

TROPICAL FOREST FACTS

- Tropical forests cover about five percent of the Earth's land surface.
- They contain over half of all living species.
- Around 1,200 species of butterfly have been recorded in one forest in southern Peru.
- Over half the world's rainforest has been cut since 1945.

IN THE CANOPY

THERE IS WARMTH, light, and plenty of food to eat in the canopy of tropical trees. The canopy provides living space for thousands of inse[c] species. In one day 3,000 different species were collected from a single tree in a forest in Borneo.

BRIGHT BEETLES
Many beetle species living on the leaves of tropical trees are brightly colored. These gaily colored beetles are difficult to see when they are sitting on shiny tree leaves in bright sunshine.

THREE LEA[F] BEETLES

-2

CICADAS
A male cicada produces a very loud mating song with drumlike organs called tymbals on both sides of its abdomen. A cavity beside each tymbal amplifies the sound. In the mating season, cicada males sing in the canopy, filling tropical forests with their shrill song.

Spines are spiked and poisonous.

FROG BEETLE

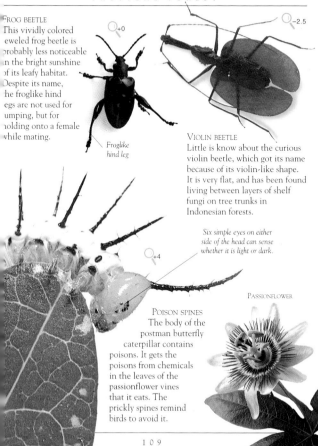

This vividly colored jeweled frog beetle is probably less noticeable in the bright sunshine of its leafy habitat. Despite its name, the froglike hind legs are not used for jumping, but for holding onto a female while mating.

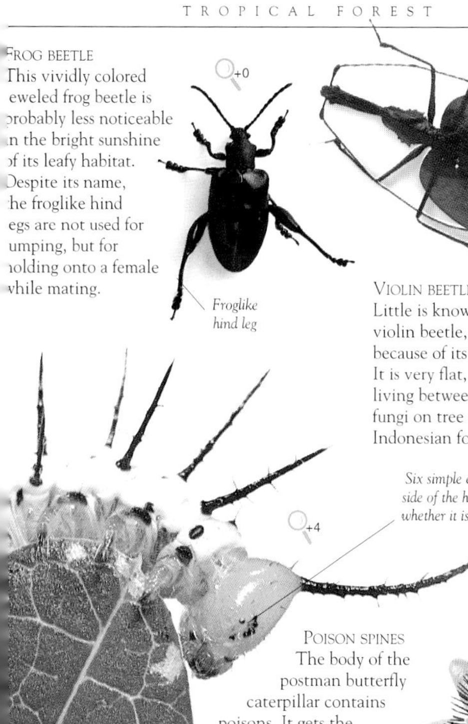

+0
−2.5
Froglike hind leg
+4
Six simple eyes on either side of the head can sense whether it is light or dark.

VIOLIN BEETLE

Little is know about the curious violin beetle, which got its name because of its violin-like shape. It is very flat, and has been found living between layers of shelf fungi on tree trunks in Indonesian forests.

PASSIONFLOWER

POISON SPINES

The body of the postman butterfly caterpillar contains poisons. It gets the poisons from chemicals in the leaves of the passionflower vines that it eats. The prickly spines remind birds to avoid it.

NESTS IN THE CANOPY

WITH SO MANY insects feeding in the forest canopy, it is not surprising that the insect-eating ants and wasps build their nests there. But these ants and wasps are in turn hunted by mammals and lizards, so their nests must give protection.

Nest is ma of paperlik material.

GREEN WEAVER ANTS

Each green weaver ant colony has several nests made of leaves. To make a nest, the ants join forces to pull leaves together and sew the edges. They sew using silk which the larvae produce when they are squeezed by the adult ants. These carnivorous ants hunt through the tree canopy, catching other insects and carrying the prey in pieces back to the ants' nests.

WASP NESTS

Each wasp species makes a different type of nest. This nes from South America has been cut in half to reveal the "floors which house the larvae. There one small opening at the botto where the wasps defend the ne from invading ants.

Ants pulling leaves together.

This nest hangs from a branch of a tree.

There may be half a million ants in one weaver ant colony.

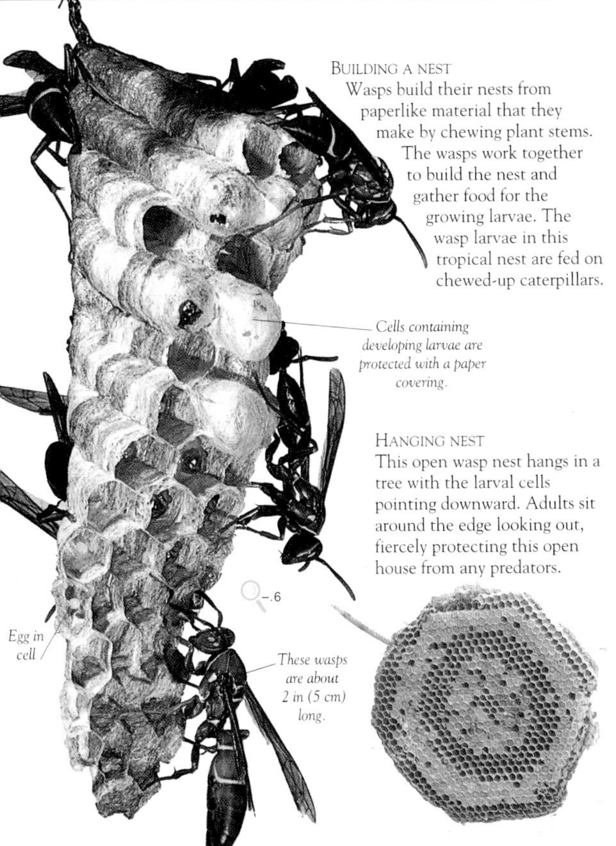

Building a nest

Wasps build their nests from paperlike material that they make by chewing plant stems. The wasps work together to build the nest and gather food for the growing larvae. The wasp larvae in this tropical nest are fed on chewed-up caterpillars.

Cells containing developing larvae are protected with a paper covering.

Hanging nest

This open wasp nest hangs in a tree with the larval cells pointing downward. Adults sit around the edge looking out, fiercely protecting this open house from any predators.

Egg in cell

These wasps are about 2 in (5 cm) long.

Brilliant Butterflies

MANY TROPICAL butterflies are large and brilliantly colored, which ought to make it easy for predators to catch them. But they fly rapidly and erratically, flash their bright color in the sun, and then seem to disappear, dartin into the deep shade of the forest.

BLUE MORPHO
The iridescent blue of South American morpho butterflies is so vivid it can be seen from a great distance. But its underwings are a muddy brown fo camouflage when feeding on the ground.

−.3

SOUTHEAST ASIAN MOTH
The vivid colors of this southeast Asian moth shows that some day-flying moths can be as colorful as butterflies. The bright colors warn predators that this moth is poisonous.

−.5

NERO BUTTERFLY
The bright yellow Nero butterfly drinks from streams and puddles near mammal dung. This habit is common in butterflies of tropical forests, and supplies them with nutrients that are not available in flowers.

+2

POSTMAN BUTTERFLY
Brightly colored and slow-flying, the postman butterfly is poisonous to predators, who quickly learn to avoid them. Groups of postman butterflies often sleep together on branches.

FEMALE BIRDWING BUTTERFLY

BIRDWING BUTTERFLIES
The males of southeast Asian birdwing butterflies differ in size, color, and behavior from the females. The brightly colored males sometimes fly near the ground, but the larger brownish females remain in the treetops.

MALE BIRDWING BUTTERFLY

TROPICAL BUTTERFLIES

THOUSANDS OF butterfly species live in tropical forests. Each butterfly has to recognize members of its own specie among all the others in order to mat They find each other by sight – butterflies have a good sense of colo and by smell.

−.6

Tail brush

USING SCENTS

Striped blue crow butterfly males have a yellow brush at the end of their abdomen. When a male has found a female, he uses his brush to dust scented scales on her. The arousing scent encourages the female to mate with him.

DETECTING SCENTS

Butterfly and moth antennae are covered in sense organs that detect scents. This is a silkmoth antenna viewed at high magnification. It is divided into segments, and each segment has two branches. The branches increase the antenna's surface area, making it more sensitive.

Branches on each segment

Scent chemicals stimulate nerves in the antennae.

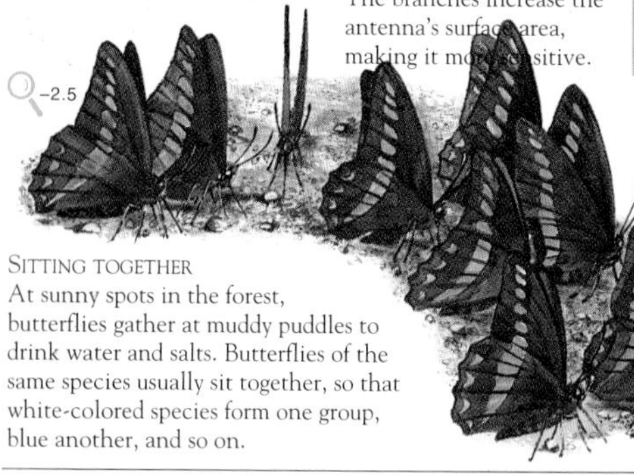

−2.5

SITTING TOGETHER

At sunny spots in the forest, butterflies gather at muddy puddles to drink water and salts. Butterflies of the same species usually sit together, so that white-colored species form one group, blue another, and so on.

Postman butterflies and small postman butterflies are two different species. But they share the same wing patterns in different parts of South America.

SMALL POSTMAN BUTTERFLY FROM SOUTHERN ECUADOR

POSTMAN BUTTERFLY FROM SOUTHERN ECUADOR

SMALL POSTMAN BUTTERFLY FROM SOUTHERN BRAZIL

POSTMAN BUTTERFLY FROM SOUTHERN BRAZIL

SMALL POSTMAN BUTTERFLY FROM WESTERN BRAZIL

POSTMAN BUTTERFLY FROM WESTERN BRAZIL

COPYING PATTERNS

Sometimes two or more different species of poisonous butterfly share the same wing pattern. This kind of mimicry means that the different species protect each other. Birds only need to learn that one species is poisonous to avoid the other.

HORNED BEETLES

WITH SO MANY millions of insects in tropical forests, individuals must sometimes compete for the best living space in which to mate and lay eggs. Horned beetles have horns which they use as weapons in battle. A male may lock horns with other males to claim a good territory, and then attract females to him.

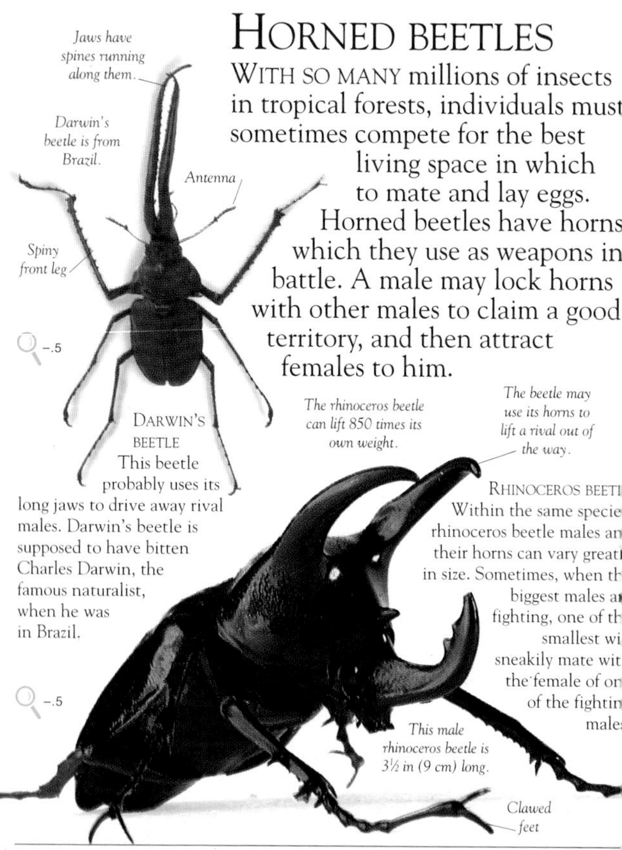

Jaws have spines running along them.
Darwin's beetle is from Brazil.
Antenna
Spiny front leg
-.5
-.5
The beetle may use its horns to lift a rival out of the way.
This male rhinoceros beetle is 3½ in (9 cm) long.
Clawed feet

The rhinoceros beetle can lift 850 times its own weight.

DARWIN'S BEETLE

This beetle probably uses its long jaws to drive away rival males. Darwin's beetle is supposed to have bitten Charles Darwin, the famous naturalist, when he was in Brazil.

RHINOCEROS BEETI

Within the same specie rhinoceros beetle males an their horns can vary great in size. Sometimes, when th biggest males a fighting, one of th smallest wi sneakily mate wit the female of on of the fightin male

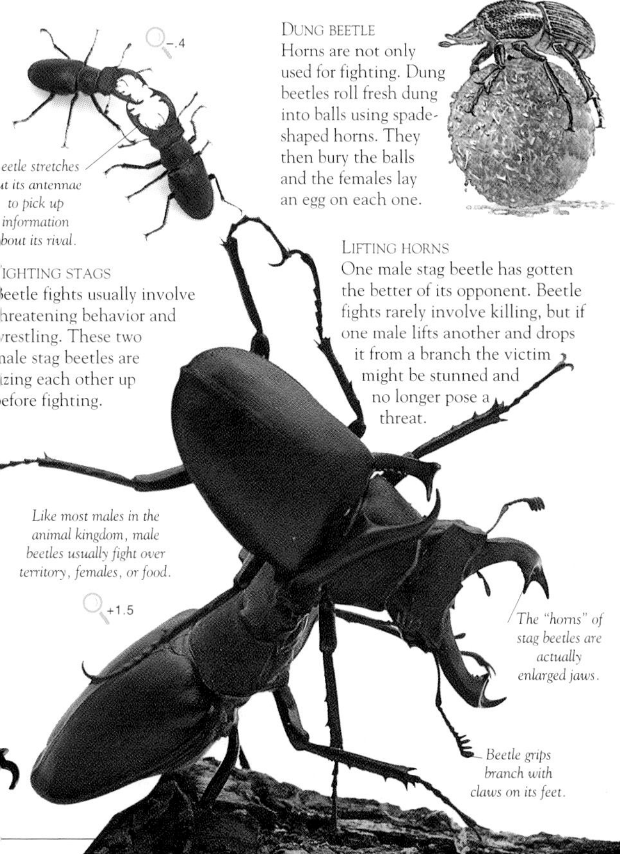

DUNG BEETLE
Horns are not only used for fighting. Dung beetles roll fresh dung into balls using spade-shaped horns. They then bury the balls and the females lay an egg on each one.

eetle stretches ut its antennae to pick up information bout its rival.

IGHTING STAGS
Beetle fights usually involve hreatening behavior and vrestling. These two nale stag beetles are izing each other up efore fighting.

LIFTING HORNS
One male stag beetle has gotten the better of its opponent. Beetle fights rarely involve killing, but if one male lifts another and drops it from a branch the victim might be stunned and no longer pose a threat.

Like most males in the animal kingdom, male beetles usually fight over territory, females, or food.

The "horns" of stag beetles are actually enlarged jaws.

Beetle grips branch with claws on its feet.

THE LARGEST INSECTS

SOME OF THE largest insects live in tropical forests, where the warm temperatures and abundance of food allow them to grow quickly. But insects cannot grow very large, since their simple breathing system could not cope with a large body. Also, big insects would be easy prey for birds and mammals.

ATLAS MOTH
With a wingspan of 6 in (15 cm), the atlas moth has the largest wing area of all insects. Silvery patch on each wing shine like mirrors.

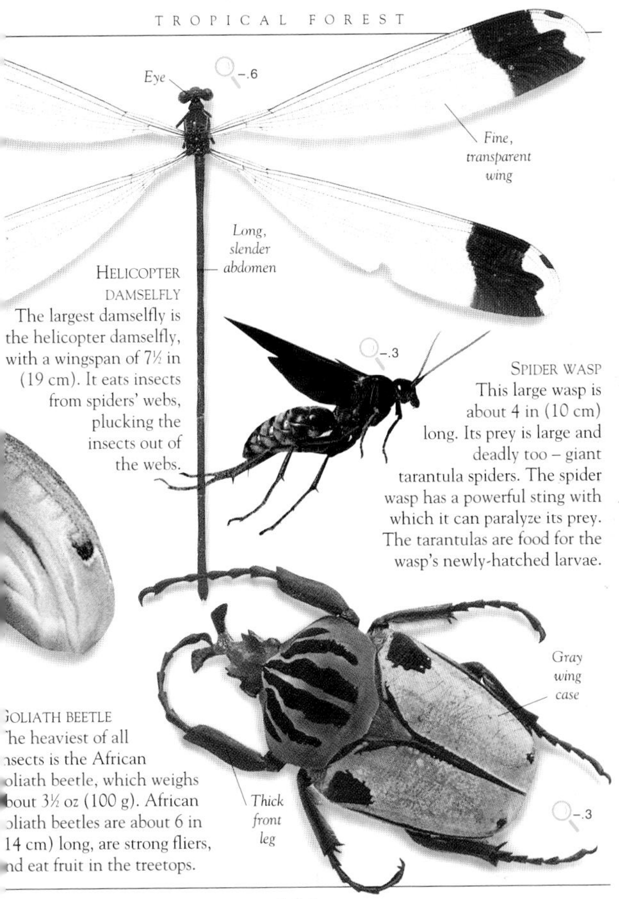

HELICOPTER DAMSELFLY
The largest damselfly is the helicopter damselfly, with a wingspan of 7½ in (19 cm). It eats insects from spiders' webs, plucking the insects out of the webs.

SPIDER WASP
This large wasp is about 4 in (10 cm) long. Its prey is large and deadly too – giant tarantula spiders. The spider wasp has a powerful sting with which it can paralyze its prey. The tarantulas are food for the wasp's newly-hatched larvae.

GOLIATH BEETLE
The heaviest of all insects is the African goliath beetle, which weighs about 3½ oz (100 g). African goliath beetles are about 6 in (14 cm) long, are strong fliers, and eat fruit in the treetops.

STICK AND LEAF INSECTS

A TROPICAL FOREST is alive with animals, most of which eat insects. To survive, insects adopt many strategies. Stick and leaf insects hide from predators by keeping still and resembling their background of leaves and sticks.

STICK INSECTS

Some stick insects are slender, brown, or green, just like the twigs and leaf stalks they sit on. Other species are shorter and fatter, with spines and other projections. These often look like curled dead leaves.

Leaf mimics

Javanese leaf insects are leaf mimics. They have body markings which look like the midrib and veins of a leaf. Brown marks like those on a dying leaf add to the disguise.

...hen resting on a branch, a ...avanese stick ...sect curls its ...ly to look like the leaves it sits beside.

Body is almost as slim as a real leaf.

Spiny stick insect

Good disguise is not just about appearance: it involves using the right behavior in the right place. This spiny stick insect is easily seen on the white background of this page. But if it were sitting in a bush and swaying gently like dead leaf, even a sharp-eyed bird may miss it.

ARMIES ON THE GROUND

ANTS ARE THE dominant creatures of tropical forests. They live in colonies made up of any number from 20 individuals to many thousands. Ants are mostly carnivorous. Some species make slaves of other ant species by invading their nest and killing their queen

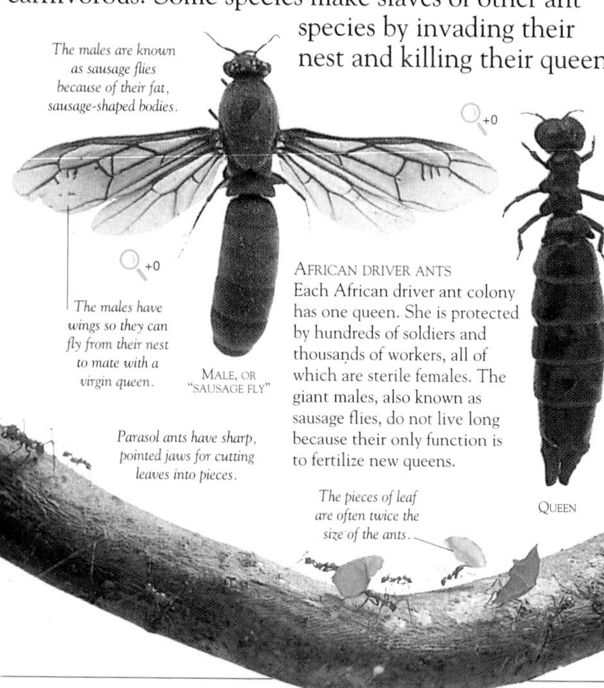

The males are known as sausage flies because of their fat, sausage-shaped bodies.

The males have wings so they can fly from their nest to mate with a virgin queen.

MALE, OR "SAUSAGE FLY"

AFRICAN DRIVER ANTS
Each African driver ant colony has one queen. She is protected by hundreds of soldiers and thousands of workers, all of which are sterile females. The giant males, also known as sausage flies, do not live long because their only function is to fertilize new queens.

QUEEN

Parasol ants have sharp, pointed jaws for cutting leaves into pieces.

The pieces of leaf are often twice the size of the ants.

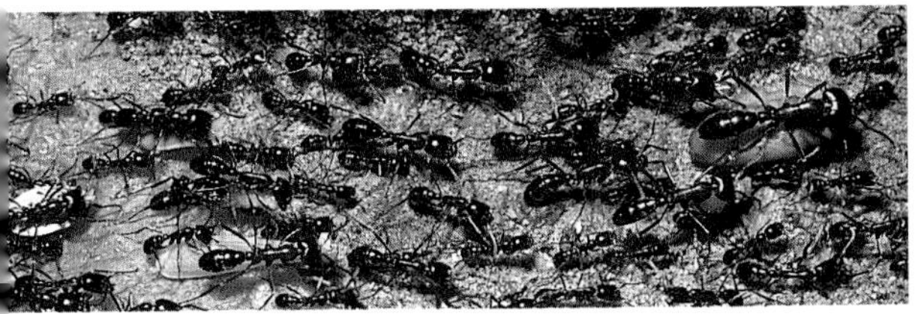

RIVER ANTS MARCHING
hese ants get their name from the way a colony
veeps through an area catching all the insects it
n find. They move their nests from place to
ace regularly, unlike most ants which have a
ermanent nest and territory.

Beetle pupae are among the prey of driver ants.

ARRYING PREY
nts in a column collaborate to cut
rge insects they have caught into
naller pieces. This is so they can carry
eir food back to the nest. Smaller
rey can be carried whole.

ATTENTIVE SOLDIER
Driver ant soldiers have very large jaws. Often they can be seen standing beside a marching column of ants with their jaws wide open, waiting to attack intruders such as parasitic flies.

Ant returning for more leaves

PARASOL ANTS
These South American ants are not carnivorous. They feed on fungus which they cultivate in huge underground nests. The fungus is grown on pieces of leaf which the ants bring to the nest.

DESERTS, CAVES, AND SOIL

SOME INSECTS flourish in habitats where it is difficult for living things to survive. Desert habitats, for example, lack water and have very high temperatures. Caves are dark and lack plant life for food. Life in soil makes communication, by both scent and sight, difficult for insects.

+4

Tiger beetle larva has hooks on body to help it climb upward.

HIDING IN SOIL

Life in the soil is only a passing phase for some insect species. This tiger beetle larva hides underground by day. At night i waits in its vertical tunnel with its jaws projecting at the groun surface, and snatches passing insects to devour in its burrov

CAVE DWELLER

This cockroach lives all its life in the dark. Like other cave creatures, it feeds on debris from the outside world. Bat dung, dead animals, and pieces of plants washed into the cave provide the cockroach with its nourishment.

:SERT BEETLE
ıe lack of water in deserts forces insects to ıd ingenious ways of obtaining moisture. This rkling beetle lives in the Namib Desert, ıere sea winds bring mists each night. The etle holds its abdomen high to catch the oisture, which then runs down into its mouth.

DESERT HEAT
The hot and dry days in deserts can lead to rapid water loss and death for animals. Most living creatures hide under stones or in the sand to avoid drying out. These animals are active at night when it is much cooler.

DESERT FACTS

- The Sahara Desert is ;preading at a rate of 3 miles (5 km) per year.
- In deserts the temperature may range rom 90°F (30°C) in he day to below 32°F (0°C) at night.
- Caves are a nearly constant temperature hroughout the year.
- 20% of the Earth's and surface s desert.

CACTUS FLOWER

DESERT PLANTS
Rain may not fall in a desert for months, or even years. Most desert plants store water so they can survive, and some desert animals rely on these plants for food. But many animals, including some insects, migrate in search of rain and the plant growth it produces.

DESERT INSECTS

HOT, DRY DESERTS are dangerous places in which to live. Animals often die from sunstroke and dehydrati (drying out). To prevent this, insects avoid the sun b staying in the shade or burrowing in the sand. Some insects have special methods of collecting water. Mar feed only at night, because the surface of the sand is too hot for them to walk on during the day.

NAMIB DESERT BEETLE
Long legs keep the body of the Namib desert beetle off the hot sand. The larvae live in the sand, scavenging on detritus (organic debris), and complete development in about six months. The adults live for several years.

DESERT LOCUSTS
Adult desert locusts fly in swarms to find fresh food. When there is enough food they breed rapidly, and huge groups of wingless nymphs hop across the desert sand.

Grasses and other plants form the diet of desert locusts.

Desert locusts get water from plant food.

TWO DESER LOCUST NYM

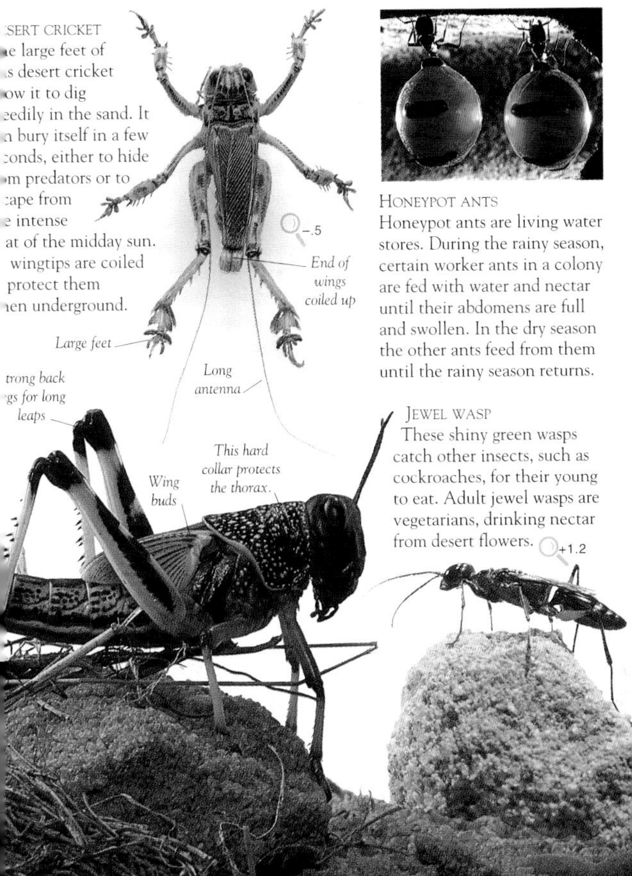

SERT CRICKET
e large feet of s desert cricket ow it to dig eedily in the sand. It n bury itself in a few conds, either to hide m predators or to cape from e intense at of the midday sun. wingtips are coiled protect them ien underground.

HONEYPOT ANTS
Honeypot ants are living water stores. During the rainy season, certain worker ants in a colony are fed with water and nectar until their abdomens are full and swollen. In the dry season the other ants feed from them until the rainy season returns.

JEWEL WASP
These shiny green wasps catch other insects, such as cockroaches, for their young to eat. Adult jewel wasps are vegetarians, drinking nectar from desert flowers.

CAVE INSECTS

ALL LIFE DEPENDS on the sun's energy. Plants change sunlight into food by a process called photosynthesis. In dark, sunless caves, nothing grows, and cave-dwelling insects must find food from outside. This food is sometimes washed in on floods, or dropped by bats and birds.

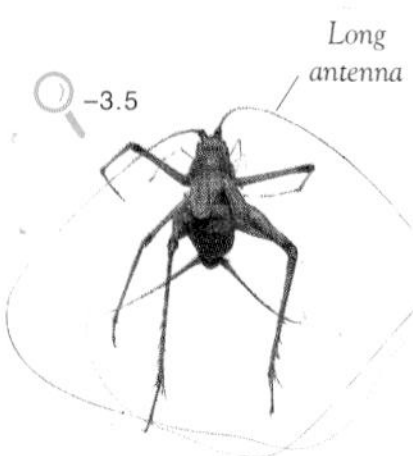

AFRICAN CRICKET
Some insects have developed very long antennae to make up for lack of vision in dark caves. This African cricket has the longest antennae for its body size of any insect.

Long back legs for jumping out of danger

FEMALE AFRICAN CAVE CRICKET

Two sensitive spines, called cerci, can detect enemies approaching from behind.

Cricket uses its ovipositor (egg-laying tube) to lay eggs in soil.

+2.5

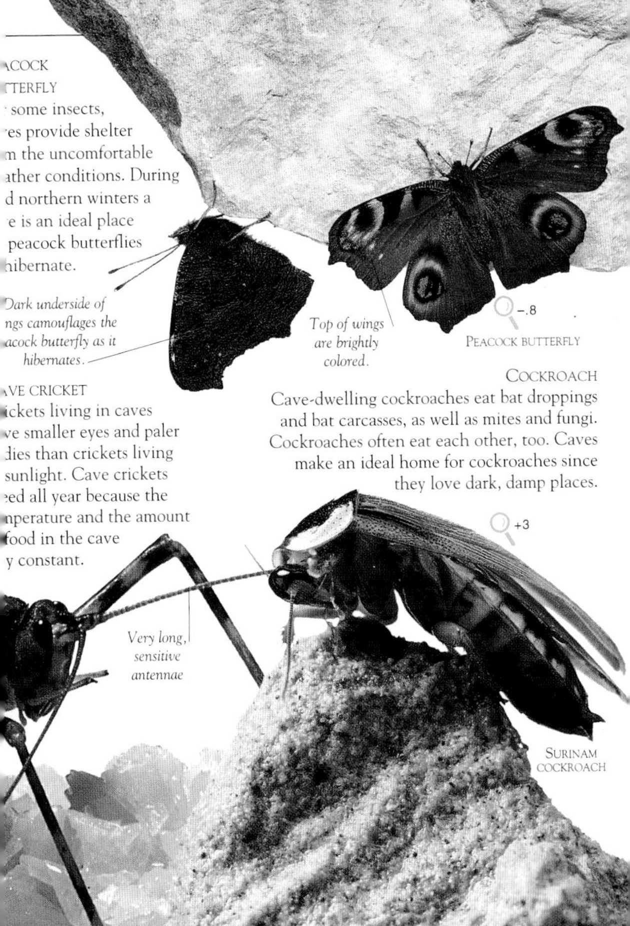

ACOCK
TTERFLY
some insects,
es provide shelter
m the uncomfortable
ather conditions. During
d northern winters a
e is an ideal place
peacock butterflies
hibernate.

Dark underside of ngs camouflages the acock butterfly as it hibernates.

Top of wings are brightly colored.

−.8

PEACOCK BUTTERFLY

COCKROACH

Cave-dwelling cockroaches eat bat droppings and bat carcasses, as well as mites and fungi. Cockroaches often eat each other, too. Caves make an ideal home for cockroaches since they love dark, damp places.

AVE CRICKET
ickets living in caves
ve smaller eyes and paler
dies than crickets living
sunlight. Cave crickets
eed all year because the
nperature and the amount
food in the cave
y constant.

+3

Very long, sensitive antennae

SURINAM COCKROACH

SOIL INSECTS

WHEN PLANTS and animals die, their remains usually get absorbed into the soil. Insects that live in soil are among the most important creatures on Earth becaus they help to recycle these remains, releasing their nutrients and so helping new crops and forests to grow. Soil insects are also an important food for many mammals and birds.

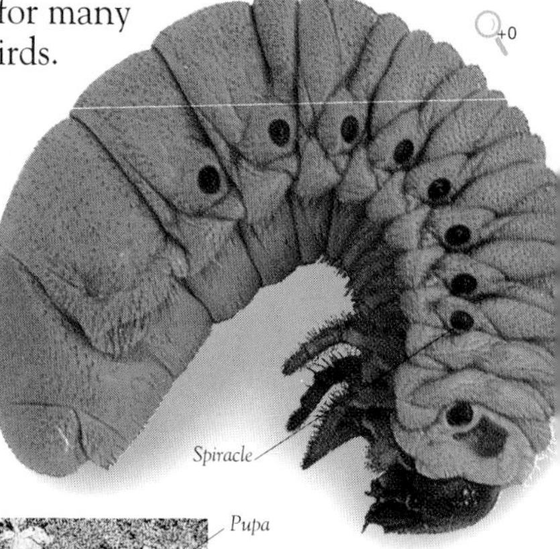

BEETLE LARVA
Roots and decaying tree trunks provide food for many types of insect larva, such as this lamellicorn beetle grub. The grub breathes through holes called spiracles, which occur along the side of its body. Although there is not very much air underground, there is enough for insects.

GOOD HABITAT
Living in soil has advantages. Inse are unlikely to dehydrate, and the is plenty of food in plant roots and decaying plants. This spurge hawk moth pupa has sharp plates on its abdomen which help it climb to th surface just before the adult emerg

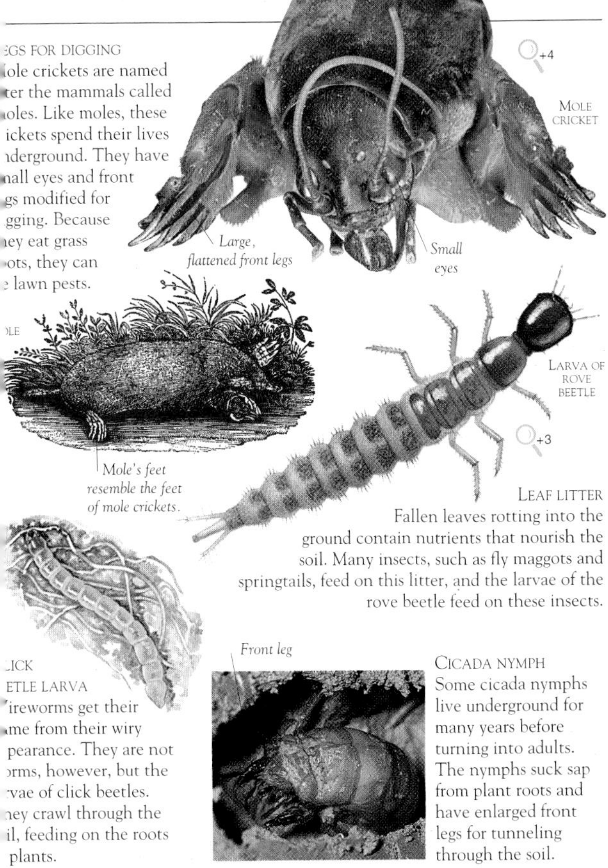

ːGS FOR DIGGING

ɩole crickets are named ter the mammals called ɩoles. Like moles, these ickets spend their lives ıderground. They have nall eyes and front gs modified for gging. Because ıey eat grass ›ots, they can ː lawn pests.

)LE

LEAF LITTER

Fallen leaves rotting into the ground contain nutrients that nourish the soil. Many insects, such as fly maggots and springtails, feed on this litter, and the larvae of the rove beetle feed on these insects.

.ICK
ETLE LARVA

'ireworms get their ıme from their wiry pearance. They are not ɔrms, however, but the ·vae of click beetles. ıey crawl through the il, feeding on the roots plants.

CICADA NYMPH

Some cicada nymphs live underground for many years before turning into adults. The nymphs suck sap from plant roots and have enlarged front legs for tunneling through the soil.

TOWNS AND GARDENS

SINCE INSECTS HAVE managed to make homes for themselves in practically every natural habitat, it is n surprising that they have turned human habitats into their homes, too. Insects live in our houses, feeding i our furniture, clothes, foodstores, and garbage dumps. Our gardens and farms are also teeming with insect life nourished by the abundance of flowers, fruits and vegetables.

Colorado beetle

−1.4

POTATO PESTS
When potatoes were brought to Europe from South America, the Colorado beetle came with them. This insect eats potato plant leaves, and can cause great damage to crops.

Leaves of potato plant

Potato

CABBAGE EATERS
Cabbage white butterflies lay eggs on cabbage plants so the larvae can eat the leaves. Farms provide acres of cabbages, and the butterflies become pests since they breec at an unnaturally hig rate because of the abundance of food.

ISECT INFESTATIONS

ests such as cockroaches are uick to make use of any food hich we waste. Uncovered or illed food in kitchens allows ese insects to thrive, and can ause an infestation that hard to eliminate.

WASPS IN OUR HOMES

The roofs of our houses keep us warm and dry, but they also provide ideal conditions for wasps' nests. Wasps are useful to us in summer since they catch our garden insect pests to feed to their young.

Nest hangs from rafters.

GREENHOUSES

In temperate countries, tropical insects often thrive in greenhouses, which reproduce tropical conditions. Butterfly farms use this principle to breed exotic insects for us to look at and enjoy.

TOWNS AND GARDENS FACTS

- More than 1,800 insect species were found in a typical English garden.
- Fewer than one percent of cockroach species are considered to be pests.
- Peacock butterflies often spend the winter in garden sheds.

The monarch butterfly is bred on butterfly farms.

HOUSEHOLD INSECTS

SINCE PREHISTORIC times, insects have lived in huma homes, attracted by warmth, shelter, and food. These insects eat our food, our furniture, and some even eat our carpets. Parasitic insects also live in our homes, feeding on the human inhabitants.

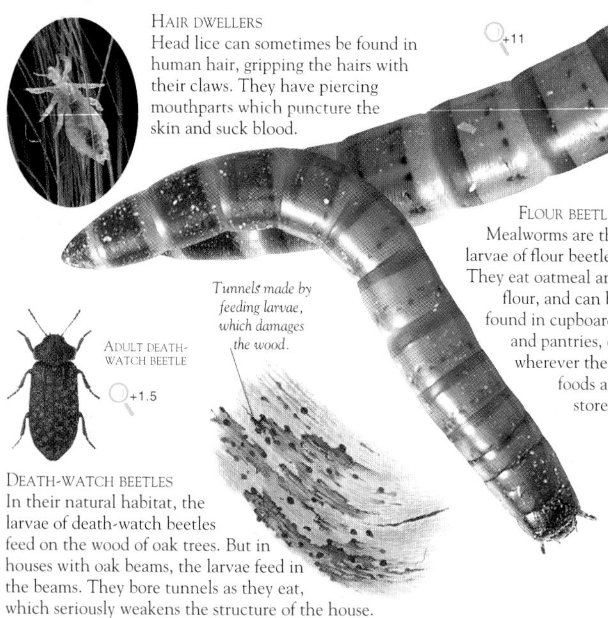
+11
Tunnels made by feeding larvae, which damages the wood.
ADULT DEATH-WATCH BEETLE
+1.5

HAIR DWELLERS
Head lice can sometimes be found in human hair, gripping the hairs with their claws. They have piercing mouthparts which puncture the skin and suck blood.

FLOUR BEETL
Mealworms are tl larvae of flour beetle They eat oatmeal ar flour, and can l found in cupboar and pantries, wherever the foods a store

DEATH-WATCH BEETLES
In their natural habitat, the larvae of death-watch beetles feed on the wood of oak trees. But in houses with oak beams, the larvae feed in the beams. They bore tunnels as they eat, which seriously weakens the structure of the house.

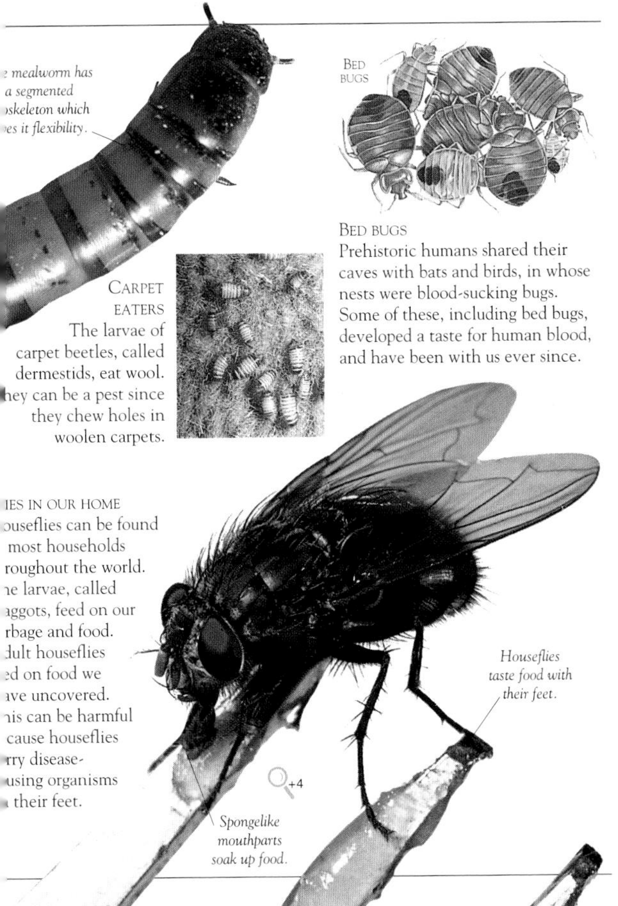

›e mealworm has
a segmented
›skeleton which
›es it flexibility.

CARPET EATERS
The larvae of carpet beetles, called dermestids, eat wool. ›hey can be a pest since they chew holes in woolen carpets.

BED BUGS
Prehistoric humans shared their caves with bats and birds, in whose nests were blood-sucking bugs. Some of these, including bed bugs, developed a taste for human blood, and have been with us ever since.

›IES IN OUR HOME
›ouseflies can be found ›most households ›roughout the world. ›ne larvae, called ›aggots, feed on our ›rbage and food. ›dult houseflies ›ed on food we ›ave uncovered. ›his can be harmful ›cause houseflies ›rry disease-›using organisms ›their feet.

Houseflies taste food with their feet.

+4

Spongelike mouthparts soak up food.

GARDEN INSECTS

A GARDEN IS a good place to watch and study insects. Many different insects are attracted into gardens to feed on the flowers, vegetables, and other plants. Som predatory insects come to eat the plant-eating insects But most garden insects are just tourists, feeding on flower nectar as they pass through.

ROVE BEETLES
Rove beetles hunt at night, scouring the garden for insects to eat. These large beetles are common in compost piles, scurrying away from the daylight when the compost is turned.

GARDENER'S FRIENDS
Hoverflies hover in front of flowe on hot, sunny days as they feed or nectar. They are particularly attracted to thistle flowers. Hoverfly larvae are the gardener's friends, feeding voraciously on plant-damaging aphids.

IINX-MOTH

e caterpillars of inx-moths can recognized by their rt, erect "tail." Most lt sphinx-moths fly at ht, hovering in front of vers to gather nectar with ir long tongues.

ARDEN GRASSHOPPER

ie common field grasshopper is widespread in rope on short grass in sunny places, and often ds a home in gardens. Like tropical locusts, mmon field grasshoppers sometimes migrate in arms, but on a much smaller scale.

OD FOR BUTTERFLIES

ie flower border of a garden is like a filling ation for passing butterflies. They feed on ctar to give them energy as they search for itable mates or plants on which to lay eggs.

FRIENDS AND FOES

THE RELATIONSHIP between insects and humans is not always good. Many insec are useful to us, although others are pests. We destroy their habitats, and deny other wild animals of food. Ecology, involving the study of the balance between our needs and the needs of other animals and plants, helps us to understand this conflict

Aphids drink the rose's sap. This may kill the rose, because the sap is like the plant's blood.

APHIDS

Aphids are major pests on our food plants and flower Some aphid species are common on roses, while others spread diseases which ruin potatoes and strawberries, as well as many other food crops.

Intricate pattern of veins in wings

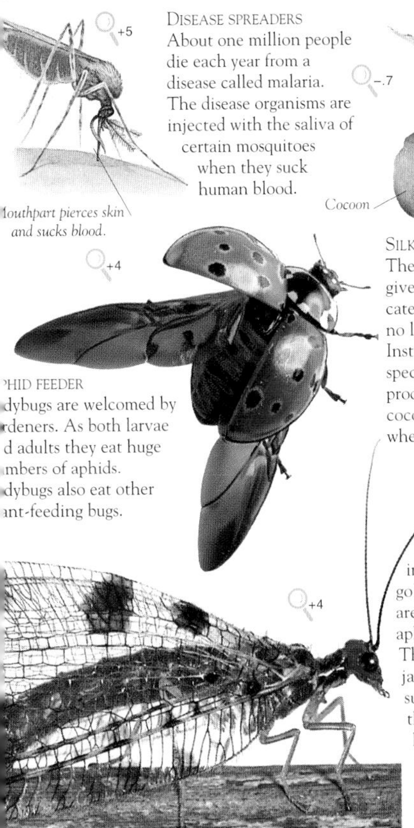

Iouthpart pierces skin and sucks blood.

DISEASE SPREADERS

About one million people die each year from a disease called malaria. The disease organisms are injected with the saliva of certain mosquitoes when they suck human blood.

−.7

Moth

Cocoon

SILK PROVIDERS

The silk we use in clothes is given to us by silkworm moth caterpillars. Silkworm moths no longer occur in the wild. Instead, they are bred in special farms. The caterpillars produce the silk to form cocoons that protect them when they pupate.

ʼHID FEEDER

dybugs are welcomed by
rdeners. As both larvae
d adults they eat huge
mbers of aphids.
dybugs also eat other
ant-feeding bugs.

PEST EATERS

Lacewings are delicate insects, often with shining golden eyes. Their larvae are voracious predators of aphids and other plant lice. They have long, tubular jaws through which they suck the body contents of their prey. Lacewing larvae hide themselves from predators by sticking the remains of their prey onto small hairs on their back.

BEES AND POLLINATION

BEES AND PLANTS depend on each other. Plants need bees to carry pollen between flowers to produce seeds Bees collect pollen and nectar from flowers to feed their larv Nectar in a hive is made into honey for winter food.

BEE-KEEPING

For thousands of years people have kept bees for their honey. Modern hives have racks of frames, each with a ready-made comb of cells. Individual frames can be removed and the honey drained.

POLLINATION

Other insects, such as butterflies, also pollinate flowers. Many flowers are a special color or shape to attract particular insects. These insects receive pollen and nectar in the process of carrying pollen to another flower.